Foxes for Everybody

Foxes for Everybody

Twenty-Four Hours of Early Motherhood

Catherine Pierce

NORTHWESTERN UNIVERSITY PRESS
EVANSTON, ILLINOIS

Northwestern University Press
www.nupress.northwestern.edu

Printed in the United States of America

10 9 8 7 6 5 4 3 2 1

Library of Congress Cataloging-in-Publication Data

Names: Pierce, Catherine, 1978– author
Title: Foxes for everybody : twenty–four hours of
early motherhood / Catherine Pierce.
Description: Evanston : Northwestern University Press, 2026.
Identifiers: LCCN 2025027547 | ISBN 9780810149533
paperback | ISBN 9780810149540 ebook
Subjects: LCSH: Motherhood | LCGFT: Essays
Classification: LCC PS3616.I347 F69 2026 |
DDC 814.6—dc23/eng/20250903
LC record available at https://lccn.loc.gov/2025027547

for S and for W

Contents

The Next Right Now

1:00 A.M.

WHAT, I WONDERED, WAS WRONG WITH ME?

Everyone—relatives, friends with older kids, people in line at the grocery store—repeated the same chorus with slightly different words. "It goes so fast." "You blink, and they're big." "Enjoy these days, because they'll be over before you know it." But these days weren't going fast, not at all. They were moving impossibly slowly. Like molasses, if molasses had been awake for nearly twenty-four hours.

Days stretched and stretched. When our newborn son woke for the morning before the sun was up, after a night that included three or four feedings, I'd count the hours until I could reasonably go to bed. If I made it until the sun went down, that would be, roughly . . . fifteen hours. Fifteen hours of diapers to change and many, many feedings and mysterious cries to decipher, plus all the regular tasks of laundry and showering, grading and course prep. This was a deflating realization to have before the sky was light.

And I was lucky—I adored my baby, delighted in him, felt lifted each time I held him. Somehow my brain's mysterious chemistry had spared me the postpartum depression I'd feared. I was just exhausted. And it was really hard. And the days went on.

And on.

And on.

It seemed impossible they'd ever go quickly. What was everyone talking about? What was I doing wrong?

At the baby shower, someone had gifted us an adorable sleepsuit, red with horses and cowboys on it. The size tag read "six months." I remember holding that giant sleepsuit next to our tiny son—born small, at five and a half pounds—when he was six weeks old and thinking that the time when he'd be able to wear it felt as remote as the time when he'd be starting kindergarten, or maybe college.

It was all so far away. Miles away, light-years, somewhere on the other side of a million days just like this, a million days that started too early and never quite ended.

By late April, a few months into parenting, the days hadn't gotten any shorter. But we'd learned how to manage them a little better, and in an attempt to find that balance between *we're parents now and everything is different* and *parenthood hasn't changed us and we're still the same people we've always been,* my husband and I, both writers and English professors in Mississippi, had accepted an invitation to give a joint reading at a college in West Virginia. It would be a little tricky with a four-month-old, but we'd make it work. Our semester ended on April 26, and we were on the road early the next morning. The plan was to drive to West Virginia over two days, do the event, then leave the morning after that and continue on to Delaware, where we'd spend part of the summer visiting family at the beach.

"The sky looks weird," said my husband. We'd been driving for a few hours. Reports had been calling for dangerous weather. The word *outbreak* was being tossed around.

"It's looked weird all day," I said, craning around into the backseat to jiggle our fussing son's toes. He was four months old, and—we were learning—not a fan of road trips.

"No, look," replied my husband, "it's got two layers." He was right: the sky was striated, a darker layer of clouds and a lighter layer, and it did look weird, or, more accurately, weirder. "I think we should pull over," he said, and turned into the parking lot of a small motel outside Cullman, Alabama.

Inside the lobby, I sat down to nurse our son while my husband checked the weather. Suddenly the door opened and in ran two women, yelling, "It's out there, it's coming!"

Everything tilted in that moment. There was an actual tornado out there. It was coming. I was holding my baby and a tornado was coming.

Everyone ran for the bathrooms, the most interior windowless space. The front desk clerk and the other patrons, all women, disappeared into the women's bathroom. My husband headed straight for the men's room, and while there's something to be said here about our bizarre and funny and troubling allegiance to gender labels even during a time of crisis—also yet another argument in favor of all-gender restrooms—what matters for the sake of this story is that, because everyone else had gone to the women's room, it was just the three of us in the men's room, just the three of us crouching against the tile wall in the corner.

I was holding our son, who was wailing, covering him with as much of my body as I could, while my husband tried to cover me. The power cut out. On the other side of the tile wall, people were screaming. *This is it,* I thought, *this is happening, this is how it ends.*

It seemed impossible. Our son was new—so, so new—and we were supposed to have years ahead of us, more than years, and suddenly time had sped up like a centrifuge and what was supposed to be a lifetime was instantly compressed to this Days Inn bathroom, this abrupt stopping. We were going to West Virginia. Our names were on flyers in the English department there—how could we vanish if our names were on flyers? It was impossible. But it was happening. A generator kicked in, bringing the lights back, but outside the bathroom the screaming didn't stop. Inside the bathroom our son kept howling.

After a few more minutes—two? ten?—we heard a woman call from the lobby that everyone could come out. The tornado had passed, she said. We stood, my legs shaking so bad that I sank into a nearby armchair as soon as we emerged from the bathroom, afraid I'd drop our son if I didn't sit right away. "I watched it go by," said the woman. "It was right there."

We couldn't stay where we were—the motel was small, plywood-flimsy—but driving for any real distance was out of the question. The clouds were still roiling. The air was thick. We knew now how foolish we'd been to travel at all with the sky like it was. We knew it so well we didn't need to say it out loud.

We'd lost phone service—we'd find out later that the cell towers in the area had been hit—so, without any concrete information to go on, we buckled our son back into his car seat and set out for the closest sturdy-looking structure we could find. We passed a wrecked gas station, its metal awning flapping like a useless limb in the wind. I scanned the sky while my husband drove. We didn't speak. Off to the right, I spotted a big chain hotel, the kind that serves free cornflakes and prefab Danish for breakfast. "There," I said, pointing, and he nodded and turned.

Inside the hotel, the power was out, as it was all across town, and the only light came through the windows and the automatic doors that had at some point been stuck in the open position. People drifted aimlessly around the lobby, up and down the halls—not travelers, we learned, but locals who had lost their homes in one of the several tornadoes that had torn through since that morning. *What have you heard?* we asked the front desk workers. But no one knew anything. Without electricity there was no internet or television, and no one had cell service. In the absence of information and updates, rumors ricocheted: Someone had heard the courthouse was gone. Someone had heard Tuscaloosa had been leveled. Someone had heard there was a huge one coming, headed directly our way.

All day, all day, the sirens sounded. Sometimes they were the warning sirens; other times they were ambulances. All day, all day, all day. When the warning blares would start up, we'd scramble under the concrete stairwell with our baby and other scared people to wait out the latest threat. Our son would cry, but I wouldn't take him out of his padded carrier during those stairwell moments—if the building got hit, he'd be more protected in there than in my arms.

We didn't know what time it was. A few people wore watches, but we didn't bother to ask. Time had ceased to make sense. It had sped up, and then it had disappeared. It didn't exist. There was no time. There was only right now, and the waiting to see if right now continued into the next right now. We couldn't let ourselves think beyond that.

I've forgotten many details about that day. Here are some that I remember:

I remember that I had two tricks that calmed my son down in the stairwell: One was to recite *Dr. Seuss's ABC* over and over ("BIG A, little a, what begins with A? Aunt Annie's alligator. A . . . a . . . A"), and the other was to sing Bob Dylan's "You Ain't Goin' Nowhere."

I remember that the stairwell had very nice acoustics.

I remember the people who crowded into the stairwell with us. I remember hoping some of them were comforted, too.

I remember writing a note to my sister, instructions on how to find a journal I'd been keeping about our son's first months in the event that he survived this but my husband and I didn't. I put the note in my purse, figuring someone would look there for identification if the worst happened.

I remember that everyone was frantic to call family and friends, but no one had reception. Finally, one guy—a guy who looked like the bully in every '80s teen movie, a guy who would have almost certainly made fun of me in junior high—got through to someone. "Could I use your phone?" I asked, and he handed it to me and then later that night my mother called me back on his phone, and he handed it to me again.

I remember that we were hungry, all of us, and there was no way to get food, until someone—the phone guy—said, "Hey, they have breakfast stuff here," and walked into the kitchen and came back with a tray of apples and bananas and muffins, and we all fell on it like animals.

I remember that much later, sometime that night, after countless cycles of stairwell crouching, the sirens stopped and we stepped outside and everything was different. There were stars. The air was cool. Cold, even. And even without weather reports or news updates, we knew it was done.

I remember that we went to the room where the trays of food were sitting, and someone had found and lit candles everywhere, and our unspeakably vast relief made that soft flickering the most beautiful thing I had ever seen.

I remember that someone gave us a flashlight, and we climbed several flights of stairs in the dark to our room.

I remember nursing our son in bed sometime after midnight, my husband sleeping next to me, while I watched the total blackness outside our window. There were no lights anywhere in the town; power wouldn't be restored for days. Once I panicked, thinking I saw a dark shape, but it was the rise of a low mountain, unmoving. My body was ringing with awareness—of the weight of our son in my arms, the warmth of my husband beside me, the three of us very, very much alive and very, very much together. My gratitude was immense. The word "gratitude" didn't scratch the surface.

The next morning, we'd drive out of town past wreckage and rubble. We'd see massive trees uprooted and on their sides. Brick buildings crumbled, roofs gone. Later still we'd learn that there was wreckage like this and worse all over the South—in Tuscaloosa, in Birmingham, in Smithville, in Cordova. We'd learn that from April 25 to April 28, the four-day stretch now termed the 2011 Tornado Super Outbreak, there were 362 confirmed tornadoes. Of those, three were EF5s, the strongest and most destructive category of tornado, all on April 27. Prior to that day, there had been no EF5s anywhere in the world for three years. Twelve of the tornadoes, including the one that hit Cullman, were EF4s. During the outbreak, 321 people throughout the South died in terrible, violent ways; thousands more were injured in terrible, violent ways; more still lost homes, lost pets and wedding photos and baby shoes and every single book and sweater and lamp and quilt.

But that night I knew none of that. That night I knew only that it was some time in the early morning. I didn't know what time it was exactly, but I could feel the minutes passing, steadily, calmly. Time had come back, and just like always, it wasn't going fast, not at all. It was slow again, and I breathed in that slowness and breathed in my baby and breathed in the possibility of the next days and weeks and months: the boardwalk fries doused in vinegar, the sharp and precise cry of the herring gulls and the summer mockery of the black-capped laughing gulls, the salt air smell, the still-dark early mornings, the diaper changes, the dinners that would get cold because of fussing or feedings, the everything-new faltering I'd do again and again, all of it, all of it. We were absurdly, obscenely lucky. There were so many minutes. There would be, somehow, so many more.

Winter Work

2:00 A.M.

I ONCE HEARD A WOMAN ON NPR TELL A STORY ABOUT flicking on her kitchen light one night to find the walls covered in cockroaches. It was a nightmarish story, but what was most terrifying to me about it wasn't the shock of the discovery, or the horror of the writhing wall. It was the fact that these cockroaches had always been there, lurking behind plaster and under floorboards, waiting for the lights to go out so they could take over.

For most of my adult life, I dreaded winter. Dreaded it. It sounds dramatic, I know. But in the winter, my own darkness multiplied and surged forth just like those cockroaches. Whatever fears—illness, accidents, loved ones dying—I'd managed to keep at bay in the warmer, brighter seasons emerged hungry and atomic-blast-proof with the early twilight.

My cockroaches loved the chill of January. They loved the way the sky, even on the brightest winter noons, was always just a little dimmer than the summertime sky. They liked to ride on my fingers as I walked through the house turning on every light, as I did in advance of each sunset. Four lamps in the living room, three in the bedroom, both hall lights, the kitchen fluorescents. It didn't matter what room I was sitting in to read or write or eat. The brighter the house, the safer I felt.

In time, though, the cockroaches stopped minding the light, and I'd find them sitting right under a circle of brightness, bold as any diurnal monster. The cockroaches, as they reminded me every winter, didn't give a shit.

The winter my husband and I decided to try for a baby, the cockroaches took over completely. They nestled in my hair while I Googled all the diseases a future child might have, all the recessive-but-fatal genetic flaws my husband and I could carry. They rested on my shoulder blades as I worked out the mathematical stats on C-section deaths, umbilical cord disasters, placental abruptions. They urged me to click on every story about a seemingly healthy child suddenly stricken with a rare deadly syndrome. In the checkout line, at the gas pump, in the shower, they hissed: car wrecks, cancers, the uselessness of odds. *Someone,* they whispered, *has to be that one in twenty thousand.*

With spring, though, the days lengthened, the air softened, and the cockroaches went semidormant again, lulled to sluggishness by heat and light and some good cognitive behavioral therapy. It was early April when I found out I was pregnant, a warm, bright day, and I was glad when I saw the two pink lines signaling *yes*. And though I had fears, sometimes big ones, my doctor was skilled and kind and willing to answer questions, and it was spring, and then summer, and then the warm Mississippi fall, and my pregnancy was full of sun, strolls under green leaves, windows thrown open to air the house after we painted the nursery its two-toned blue.

But my son was due in mid-December, a few days before the longest night of the year. I knew the warmth wouldn't hold. And everyone—*everyone*—had told me the up-all-night horror stories. Those stories haunted me. Not because I feared the sleep deprivation, but because I dreaded a wintertime darkness with even more muscle than the ones I'd fought through for years.

Sometimes, seven or eight months pregnant, I would wake in the night to use the bathroom and would peer through the slats in the blinds to the black sky outside, the stars sharp and cold through the trees. When the baby was born, those trees would be bare. When the baby was born, that blackness would be colder. I felt a terrible anticipatory loneliness in those moments.

I knew what it was like to be isolated in my own head. What would it be like in winter, awake in that dark silent house, holding a baby I couldn't even imagine?

I'd always thought of the deepest part of night as *the witching hour,* a time, my childhood books had taught me, that was not for humans. In a month or so, I'd see the witching hour again and again. And the cockroaches would know my human self had no place there.

Then my son was born. And what shocked me most—more than the surprising goriness of my body's healing, more than the strange sounds newborns make, more than the ferocity of my nursing-mother appetite—were the nights. Those long, dark, cold winter nights I had feared more than childbirth itself. They became something I hadn't known a night could be: a haven. A shelter.

When our son finally fell asleep, my husband and I would go to bed ourselves, the silence of our house suddenly sacred, fragile as blown glass. And when, after an hour or two, our son would wake again and cry, I'd hold him in the soft rocking chair, nurse him there in the nightlight's glow. Sometimes I'd surf the internet on my phone, feeling a companionable affection for anyone posting on Facebook in the wee hours; sometimes I'd just sit there, half in dreams. My son would fall asleep, and I'd know I should try to get some more sleep myself, but often I'd hold him a little longer, the heavy sleeping weight of him, the warmth of him in his soft flannel zippered pajamas against the chill of the January night. The silence a globe around us.

I stopped minding when the sun dropped below the trees at 5 P.M. I was exhausted by then, and it felt right that the day should be ending. And when the full dark came and wrapped itself around our house, the darkness felt like a cave, safe and ancient. I felt my animal self stir and settle. The night let me burrow deep in my new life. The night unthreaded me from human time, human brain. There was a baby, and there was my body, and there was food and shelter and the warmth of the other bodies in this shelter. There were cockroaches sometimes, too, but I couldn't be bothered with them, not for long.

I was a bear, a bobcat, a wolf. I was large and furred. I was going on instinct.

When something crawled across me, I let it, then got back to tending. I was busy with the work of winter.

It wasn't that everything was suddenly easy. My anxiety didn't disappear, of course. There was an abundance of it (suffocation, choking, a new set of worries—torticollis, RSV, infant botulism—in which I quickly became expert), and there still is. I lose hours to it sometimes, disappear down the rabbit hole as I always have. The sleep deprivation was disorienting and seemingly endless. And I had absolutely no idea what I was doing.

But since my son's birth, more than a decade ago now, I haven't once dreaded the end of daylight saving time, that autumn date that confiscates sixty minutes of gold-light evening. Now when I see it approaching on the calendar, I feel a little ping of glad anticipation. These days, winter means an excuse to stay in. It means a harking back to those early weeks. It means—unbelievably—comfort. Winter is dark, but now it's a darkness I want to climb inside.

One evening that first February of my son's life, it snowed, unusual for Mississippi. At 2 A.M. I held my son in his rocker. Outside, the moonlight and streetlights on the snow turned the sky a glowy gray orange. The neighborhood was silent, blanketed in its unexpected whiteness. It was the witching hour again. I'd been right: it was not a time for humans. It was a time for my son and me, two animals warm against the cold world outside. And it was a time for that world, too deep in the work of winter to pay us any mind.

Narrative Theory

3:00 A.M.

THE STORY I WANTED TO TELL WAS THE ONE ABOUT our son's perfect third birthday. How we'd traveled smoothly from Mississippi to Pennsylvania (with the usual travel-with-a-toddler challenges, sure, but in the story I wanted to tell, we'd handled them easily and with admirable good humor) and settled in at his grandparents' house; how he slept snugly and soundly on his last night as a two-year-old (a tidy conclusion to his early years of terrible sleeping); and then how, on his birthday, we'd taken him to the long-promised children's museum, where he'd spent the day climbing and exploring and learning and generally demonstrating excellent fine and gross motor skills. In the story I wanted to tell, I'd be that most admirable pregnant mother—the one who, even with her growing belly, has limitless warmth and energy, more than enough to make her child's birthday Very Special. There would be cupcakes and hugs, and at the end of the day, sleepy in a good way, we'd all go peacefully to bed.

That was the way it was supposed to go. But by the time our son woke on his birthday morning at a little before 3 A.M., we were already well outside the success zone. The flight had been a nightmarish experience—a winter storm had whipped up while we were in the air, and after an hour of jolting and bouncing and dropping and some shrieking (me), our plane was rerouted to a small regional airport in Allentown, Pennsylvania, where we rented a car and drove three and a half hours white-knuckled through whiteout conditions. Our son, being potty-trained, utterly refused to pee in any public bathroom, which added a dose of time-sensitive desperation to our travels. Then, when we'd finally, finally arrived at my mother and stepfather's house outside Philadelphia, we learned that the children's museum we'd been talking up for weeks as a special birthday outing would be closed tomorrow, as it was every Monday—it hadn't occurred to us to check. By the time we crashed into bed that night, we were exhausted, and more than a bit demoralized.

So when our son woke up at a time that could only very generously be counted as "morning," I was desperate to believe he just needed a reset before conking out again. After all, he'd become pretty good at sleeping through, and it had been an epic day of travel, and surely, surely this was just a blip in a long night of much-needed rest. "Shh," I said, "we're at Mom-Mom's and Pop-Pop's. Good night, buddy." I rubbed his back for a minute then gently pulled my hand away, hoping he was asleep.

He was not asleep. By 3:15 I was holding him in the rocking chair, singing the Darlene Love version of "Winter

Wonderland," complete with, at his request, the whoa-oh-ohs in the final chorus. The lights were still off. I was singing quietly. I was trying, I was trying, I was trying. Surely he would sleep soon. He was still now, snuggled against my shoulder, and I finished the song, hoping I'd lullabied him to sleep. He lifted his head. "Again!" he said. Finally, after an hour of singing and rocking, of shh-ing, of quiet calm reading by a dim lamp, I made a considered parenting choice: I gave up.

There are so many rules in parenting. So many books and magazine articles and blog posts, so many stories from friends and aunts and cousins and coworkers. And the rules are the same but also just a little different or maybe completely different depending on who you talk to, and it's all so confusing and exhausting, but the one thing you know is that there are rules. The three-year-old isn't supposed to start the day at 3 A.M. The parents aren't supposed to screw up the birthday plans. Certainly the mother isn't supposed to give in and let her toddler run the show. Consistency is key. Routine, routine, routine.

I knew all of this. But what routine? What consistency? If the day before had been spent in the sky during a snowstorm, why couldn't our son decide that today the morning would start in the middle of the night? I flicked on the overhead lights and took out of the closet whatever toys didn't beep or ding or talk—the wooden shape sorter, the cardboard bricks. Outside it was icy black, but this was morning now. It was morning because our son had decided it was morning, and so it was. It felt better, accepting awakeness instead of trying to exist in that liminal twilight state of conscious-enough-to-be-in-charge and half-asleep-enough-to-go-back-to-bed.

I'd wanted the story to be about success: an easy travel day navigated by savvy, good-natured parents; a joyous birthday at a long-promised destination. When the storm hit, I'd revised, but my new version of the story would be even better because it had conflict to overcome; the new version would be about how we'd made it through a harrowing trip and then still given our son a wonderful birthday. About the magic of the snow, how he'd seen house after house of Christmas lights from our rented car and didn't realize his parents were afraid. I didn't want the story to be about how we screwed up and forgot to see if the museum was open. I didn't want it to be a story about how we were so tired we couldn't have breakfast with him on his birthday, about how, at 5:30 A.M., entirely spent, we handed him over to his very generous grandmother, who took care of pancakes while his dad and I went back to sleep for a couple of hours.

But for a little while that early, early morning, I gave up on the story. I was too tired to tell it, anyway.

Seeing the light under the door, my husband came in, silently assessed the situation, and sat on the floor with us. It was our son's birthday. We were exhausted, and our son was happy though he'd be exhausted later, and we were happy even while we were exhausted, and all of these things could be true at once. The whole thing—not just this very early morning, but all of it, all of it—was too big for a single narrative. The flight had been absolutely terrifying and also absolutely okay because no one had been hurt. Our son's cardboard bricks, the quietest of the quiet toys, made a tremendous and satisfying racket as he toppled his tower over. We were tired. We might never not be tired, ever again, ever ever ever, with this child who didn't like sleeping and a new baby arriving in a few months. We could be tired and glad at the same time. Not glad about being tired, but glad alongside being tired. We could do that. We could sit on the floor and build with our son. We could give up and let the story happen.

A Small Defense of Screen Time

4:00 A.M.

MY OLDEST SON, FOUR AT THE TIME, HAD WOKEN up too early again. It was chilly, and dark, and I was desperate to stay just a little longer in the cocoon of sleep, so I hauled him into bed with my husband and me and fumbled with the phone, pulling up an episode of a cartoon he liked featuring a team of ocean-exploring animals. It's an educational show, which is what I was telling myself as I handed him the phone and rolled back over.

The episode filtered in and out of my dozing. I saw the sea, first cartoon blue then dark and actual, something I was floating through. The episode seemed to be about a jellyfish that, when threatened, could revert to its baby self and begin life again, over and over. It would never die. In my half dreams, my son warm beside me, the bedroom flickering softly from the phone's small screen, this made sense.

Later that day, as I worked in my fluorescent-lit office, my mind kept returning to this impossible thing I'd invented. I thought I could explain it: who, in that predawn tableau, wouldn't dream about staying forever? Still, it had seemed so real. It gnawed at me as I graded papers, met with students, returned emails. Finally, feeling foolish, I Googled "immortal jellyfish."

And there it was: *Turritopsis dohrni*. According to Wikipedia, it is a "small, biologically immortal jellyfish found in the Mediterranean Sea and in the waters of Japan." They revert to a juvenile stage again and again until eaten by predators. If they manage to elude predators forever, they will, theoretically, never die.

Sometimes the facts of the world, which seem most days tall and solid as skyscrapers, reveal themselves as nothing more than shadows painted painstakingly onto a scrim. When I read "biologically immortal," a tiny rip appeared in the base of what I'd known as, perhaps, the most solid of all facts. There was a light coming through that tear. I couldn't put my eye to it—it was too bright—but in its glow, my office rippled and swam. If this, what else? I knew I wouldn't live forever. I knew that no one I loved or didn't love would, either. But something tiny and wispy and moon-translucent might swim through the dark blue endlessly. Inside that knowledge, I could almost float.

An Incomplete Catalog of My Vigilance

5:00 A.M.

"Bird, your life would terrify me."

—Nicky Beer, "Cardinal Virtue"

1

The mother cardinal had built her nest stealthily—none of us had seen her flying back and forth to the holly bush by our front door, carrying small twigs and pine needles, shaping them into a perfect bowl the size of my two cupped hands. But just after sunrise that May morning, there she was: a small, brown bird, her orange beak the only bit of brightness sparking from inside the dark of the glossy leaves.

My sons were thrilled. Honestly, so were my husband and I. The nest was no more than two feet from the window next to our door—we could peep out any time we wanted.

"When will the eggs hatch?" my older son asked.

"I don't know," I replied. "We'll just have to watch."

And we did. We peered at the nest whenever we got the chance. If I was carrying a pile of folded towels to the bathroom closet, I checked on the bird. My sons would hop up from the dinner table, run to the door just to see what was happening, and then return to their spaghetti. Sometimes I'd use the bird as a distraction—"Hey, guys, go see if the eggs are hatching," I'd call when I could hear the brotherly tussling reaching a dangerous pitch, and they'd dash to the door, the scuffle momentarily forgotten.

We tried to take pictures of the cardinal through the window, but they never turned out. Through the glass pane and deep in the leaves' shadow, she was always a formless blur, even with the good camera. And if we dared get close enough to focus in: a quick flutter, and she was gone.

The cardinal seemed never to sleep. Whenever we approached the window, she would spot us and tense. She flew away every time I walked past her to enter the house, even when I parked at the other end of the driveway and muted my keys inside my palm as if they were a bell's clapper, turned my head away, unlocked the front door with nothing more than a click. I couldn't fool her. She was always on the alert.

2

I've been vigilant for as long as I can remember. As in deep dives into any awful potentiality. As in what's this cough about, this node, this twinge, this lump? As in second opinion, third opinion, X-ray, ultrasound. As in six medical tabs open at once on the laptop and toggling back and forth to compare. As in what are the odds of *x* cancer at *y* age? What are the risks underlying this recommended screening, this standard treatment? As in a head full of statistics and constant calculations: *one in 280, one in twenty-five thousand, one in a million, and I lived in Columbus, Ohio, for three years and a million people lived there and I was one of them and I wasn't invisible at all.* As in, *Have you done everything, absolutely everything, that you can?* As in lost Junes. Blurred highways. Invisible aspen. Days hazed and gone inside the wakefulness of worry.

3

Predators of cardinals include owls, hawks, snakes, and domestic cats, all of which my neighborhood has. Cardinal eggs are at risk of being eaten by squirrels (also plentiful in my yard), blue jays, owls, and hawks. Many cardinals never make it to the hatching stage, and if they do, their world is rife with hazards. Our holly bush is spiky—my kids call it *the prickly tree*—and in the spring it's home to wasps we can never seem to get rid of. I admired the cardinal's choice to make her nest in this inhospitable place. To put whatever barriers she could between her eggs and the yard of threats.

4

In high school, I had a friend—we'll call him Henry—who, sunk deep in depression, had taken to driving around after downing some of his parents' bourbon. I worried for Henry. But more than that, I worried for my parents and my sister. My fear was vivid, utterly real, and unshakably specific: they'd be out driving—maybe my father bringing my sister home from a softball game, or my mother running to the grocery store—and Henry, in my paralyzing daydreams, would swerve drunk through a red light and kill them. Why was this the only scenario I imagined, instead of any of a thousand other possible outcomes? Because the idea of it—the death of my family at the hands of my friend—was unbearable. Because even more unbearable was my knowledge that, if it happened, it would be my fault. I'd have my own lack of vigilance to blame. I hadn't stopped it, hadn't even tried other than a half-hearted talk with Henry, who brushed me off. I couldn't bring myself to rat him out to his parents or to mine, though I knew I should. I hadn't done everything I could. It was the single worst thing I could imagine, and so I imagined it. I imagined it so much that it felt like a likelihood. Each night I carried my guilt to bed with me, lay down with it on my chest.

5

The first time I saw the cardinal tense—body suddenly primed for flight, eyes unblinking—I recognized myself. It was almost shocking, the uncanny instant connection I felt. *Hello,* I thought. *I know you.* I knew the assigned kinship was absurd and unreciprocated—the cardinal didn't see me as anything other than a threat, which of course I was. Still, I felt a flash of tenderness for the bird. For her fear of me. For her bright, suspicious eye.

6

If you dig deep enough, you'll find that almost every edible thing is potentially dangerous for a pregnant woman. I knew to avoid soft cheeses, sushi, raw batter. I hated sprouts, so those were no loss. But the more I read—and I read and read—the more complicated it got. Bottled Caesar dressing was fine, but if the restaurant made its own in-house, there was the threat of uncooked egg. Soft ice cream was a no-go because the machines could harbor listeria. Fish containing high mercury levels were off-limits because of the risk to the unborn baby's brain and nervous system—but it's equally important to eat *some* fish so the omega-3 fatty acids can aid in brain development. The FDA offers an elaborate, color-coded chart categorizing kinds of fish as "best choice," "good choice," or "choice to avoid," and advises that pregnant women "eat 2 to 3 servings of fish a week from the 'Best Choice' list OR 1 serving from the 'Good Choice' list." The summer I was pregnant with my first son, I tucked a copy of that chart into my purse so that I could easily refer to it when ordering in restaurants. When possible, I ordered salmon—one of the universally recommended "safe" fish during pregnancy—until I found out that "salmon" was a broad category. Wild-caught Alaskan salmon was safe, but Atlantic salmon was overfished and frequently contaminated. Or so said one website, or another one.

At an autumn party, I didn't drink the cider in case it was unpasteurized. At Thanksgiving, I didn't eat the stuffing; if baked inside the turkey, it can pick up bacteria. I skipped salad bars. I avoided pineapple because it contains bromelain, which is rumored to thin the cervix. I didn't drink even decaf coffee for fear of an increased risk of miscarriage. The medical website I'd read was clear that only excessive caffeine intake—described as three or more cups of regular coffee per day—could cause a problem, but for me, it was a no-brainer: if safety was a choice, I was going to choose it, every time.

7

The more I watched the cardinal, the more I tried to come to some sort of peace with the anxiety our human presence seemed to cause her. *She's a bird,* I muttered to myself one afternoon as she flew off again when I unlocked the door. *It's okay, this is just her life*. If it wasn't my sons with their noses against the glass, my husband with his iPhone, me with my keys, it would be a cat, a hawk, a jay. At least, I told myself, we wouldn't eat her, or steal her eggs. I even tried murmuring something to that effect to the cardinal as I approached, soothingly, like I would talk to a child or a frightened dog, but she wasn't interested in my reassurances.

8

Aluminum, hard plastics, soup cans, sunscreen, lip gloss, lotion, nail polish. Parabens, phthalates, toluene, DBP, BPA, BHA, rBST. Breast cancer, colon cancer, Alzheimer's, reproductive toxicity, asthma, cognitive function. The threats blur and blur.

I try to steer closer to savvy awareness than obsession. My kids eat the blue ice pops. I buy the iridescent topcoat on a whim without checking the ingredient list. But I've also disappeared into tunnels of research, scouring website recommendations to find the least-harmful-but-still-affordable sunscreen for my family, messaging with customer service reps about the potential toxicity of a loveseat's upholstery. Last summer, after reading a clickbait article about how women ingest seven pounds of lipstick in their lifetime, I found myself in a salon inspecting tubes of bright glosses billed as "the first edible lipstick." I'd fact-checked the article. I knew it was bunk. Even so, when I saw the pinks and plums and peaches with their bamboo applicators, I thought, *Have I done everything I can?*

9

The shade I bought is called Deeply in Mauve, and it looks great.

10

It's foolishness, of course, to graft my human fears onto the bird, to use her as some kind of foil for myself. I knew—I know—a bird is a bird, and to pretend otherwise strips both bird and human of some essential part of themselves. The cardinal was nothing like me, not really. Here I was, with my human worries and privileges, my high-speed internet, my cataloguing of threats, my twenty-four-hour news cycle, my well-built house with a heavy front door and solid deadbolt, my health care benefits, my options upon options. And here was the bird, engaged in the work of hatching her eggs, keeping them warm. I nearly wrote "her single-minded work," but how do I know the bird's mind? I don't. I only know that it isn't the same as mine.

Still, each time she flinched, I saw myself.

Narcissism, I know, is also human.

11

Having lived in Mississippi for fifteen years, I've learned to monitor the weather. I watch for drastic temperature drops, for predicted changes in barometric pressure. I know how to read the radar and have learned that rotation in Yazoo City means that soon enough the same cell will likely make its way to our town. I keep an eye on the TOR:CON, an index that shows the risk of tornadoes in a specific area on a given day. When I step outside and the air feels heavy and thick and the trees are flashing their leaves' pale underbellies, I trust my instincts. And if I'm getting the kids ready for school on a bad weather day—the sky maybe still blue, but something coming, either predicted or felt—I lay out the red-striped T-shirt for my younger son, the bright yellow uniform polo for his brother. I've watched enough documentaries about tornadoes to know that, in the event of wreckage, it's the people who are spotted who survive.

12

Other days, though, I make the opposite decision about clothing. Some days—after the Uvalde shooting, for example, or the Marjory Stoneman Douglas High School shooting, or the Santa Fe High School shooting, or the Sutherland Springs shooting, or Las Vegas, or Orlando, or Roseburg, Oregon—I lay out the muted grays and beiges for my boys. I don't want to imagine school as a potential war zone, but I understand the benefits of camouflage.

13

One afternoon, I peeked at the nest and saw the cardinal with her mouth agape, panting like a dog. My heart dropped—was she sick? Injured? Was there something I should do?

I turned immediately to Google, where I found that some species of birds, when they're very hot, cool themselves by using what's called "gular fluttering"—an open-mouthed shuddering of the neck muscles that helps promote heat loss. It was a Mississippi afternoon in May; temps had reached the low nineties. The bird was doing what she needed to do. She didn't need my concern.

14

Whenever I teach in a new classroom, as I do many semesters, I make a quick scanning assessment of what could be stacked against the door, what could be slammed against a skull. At least once per class period—always, every class period, every semester—a yell in the hallway, a shadow past the classroom window, a shriek from the campus quad outside makes me consider, silently and somewhere behind my lecture about line breaks, how quickly I could move, how fast I could shepherd and rally my students, if the gunshots came.

One morning I was getting ready for work and saw that one of my sons had put a toy car inside my school bag—a bright pink Volkswagen that my oldest had chosen from a bookstore display when he was two. It was metal and heavy, the size of a hamster. I took it out, ready to return it to the toy bin—and then considered its heft, how neatly it fit into my palm, how its impact could momentarily stall an intruder. *Put as many barriers as you can between yourself and the threat,* urged our required Active Shooter Training Module. I put the car back into my bag, more totem than weapon, maybe, but there, nestled alongside the dry-erase markers and binder clips.

15

The bird outwitted all of us, in the end, or at least she outlasted us. At the end of May, when the boys' school year ended, we left for our long-planned summer travels—Colorado for the kids' first hiking adventure, then Delaware for an extended visit with grandparents and friends and the Atlantic Ocean. The eggs must have hatched—I'm hoping—soon after we headed out of town. At any rate, when we arrived back home, late one August evening, the bird and the eggs were gone. Despite all our watching, we'd missed it.

I know the mother could have fallen prey to a cat, the eggs could have been eaten by a squirrel or blue jay. According to the Cornell Lab of Ornithology, only 15 to 37 percent of nests end up with juvenile birds who live long enough to fledge. I know that though cardinals mate for life, I never saw this female's partner, which made me worried about his fate.

I know, too, that vigilance only counts for so much. A semi blows a tire and swerves into the Honda. The mammograms are clear year after year and then one morning a splintering pain at the skull's base. A storm rocks the nest. A hawk makes a dive. Ball game cheers shatter into popping.

I know all this. Still, when we got back from our trip and found the nest empty, the bird gone, I let myself imagine that what I'd hoped would happen did: the clutch of eggs hatching just after another sunrise, the dawn still soft. Small, gray, naked nestlings with their mouths open wide. The father—not absent after all, just stealthy—bringing them grubs, bringing beetles for the mother. A quiet front door, finally, no one jangling in or out. The juveniles testing their legs and wings, and then each bird fledging, all that work, all that watchfulness leading to this, the just-dark summer evening with its bounty of crickets and cicadas and golden orb-weaver spiders, the air thick with the hum of survival.

Existentialism

6:00 A.M.

"WHY DID THE HORSEY CROSS THE ROAD?" ASKED THE little one, who had recently begun the yearslong apprenticeship to logic that joke telling requires. It was early, the dark gray sky streaked with pink, and I was fumbling with the coffeemaker.

"I don't know, why?" I replied.

"Because he was running out of time," he said. And we both laughed and laughed.

When our oldest was in preschool, he was curious about everything. He had constant questions. *What comes after space? Is Cookie Monster a boy or a girl? Can my tummy hear? Why are there wheels in the world?* I loved his questions, loved learning how his brain worked, loved imagining what it must be like to experience things—wheels, Muppets, the concept of space—for the first time. Then one evening after dinner, when he was almost four, he said, "What time will my body stop working?"

It took me a second to register what he was asking, and then I got it. "Do you mean when will you not be alive anymore?" I asked. I couldn't say the word "die," not yet.

"Yes," said my son, and I said, "Not for a very long time," and then he asked if I'd still be with him when he wasn't alive, and it was then that I felt it in my solar plexus, like someone had sucker punched me with an invisible fist. I started rambling, unprepared, assuring him, trying to explain the concept of heaven without necessarily committing to it, feeling like my insides were dissolving, and then—

"Look, a coin!" said my son, pulling a dime out of the couch cushion where he'd been digging. It was shiny. I told him he could keep it.

I can distill my parenting ethos to a few key tenets, and chief among these are *Offer comfort* and *Be honest*. I want my children to know that they can talk to me, that I'll listen to them, that I'll love them, always, no matter what, that I'll try to make things better when I can. And I want them to know that they can trust me. I've always had a policy of being truthful with my children; I may keep certain details quiet, or downplay them, or otherwise try to make a difficult thing something a child can digest, but if my kids ask me a question, I do my best to answer honestly.

In retrospect, I marvel at the hubris I'd held up until that moment—*It's not that hard to be truthful*, I'd thought, *if early on you normalize the facts*. Where babies come from. Why the grandparents are divorced. The names of all the parts of the body. What that word means, and why you can't say it around your teacher. *Easy,* I thought, *information is neutral.*

But that was before my son asked me when he'd die, before he asked if I'd still be with him after he did. There was nothing neutral about it. It was breath-sucked-out-of-me, very emphatically not neutral. And suddenly my parenting compass was spinning, magnetic north lost, comfort and truth suddenly and fiercely at odds.

The next time death came up, a couple of months later, my son's focus had shifted: this time he asked what time *I* wouldn't be alive anymore. I assured him that most people don't die until they're old ("Like seventy or eighty?" asked my son; "Yes," I replied, "and some live even longer, and some die earlier, but most people don't die until they're old," clunkily trying to fit it all in), and this satisfied him for a few hours, until later that night when he brought it up once more, worrying that when I died, he'd be, in his words, "all alone."

I did my best. I told him he'd never be alone because he'd always have people who loved him. I said things like, "Some people believe there's a place called heaven, where you see your loved ones again after they die" and "everyone dies, but it's natural and it isn't scary" and "I'm young and healthy and that won't happen for a very long time" (silently praying *please please* to the god I didn't know if I believed in) and "even after I'm gone, I'll still be with you" (in retrospect, maybe both confusing and worrying to a four-year-old just getting familiar with the concept of ghosts). And eventually I threw enough words his way that he was satisfied, or satisfied enough, or maybe just bored, and we moved on.

We're not a religious family. I grew up sporadically attending a Presbyterian church and then grew increasingly wary of organized religion as I got older. My husband is Jewish, and his own wariness matches or surpasses mine; we've only ever been to temple for the bar mitzvahs of our nephews and friends' kids. We embrace the traditions of our respective backgrounds. We celebrate Christmas and Chanukah, we hide Easter eggs and the afikomen, we gather with family to share holiday meals, and we tell the stories of our inherited faiths as exactly that—stories, like any legend passed down over time. I have questions, and fears, and sometimes I miss the easier certainty of my youth, but I've mainly made my peace with the fact that, for me, the answer to big questions of faith and God and death is always the same: *I don't know*.

Within a handful of years, the little one had lots of questions of his own. What happens when people die, and when will it happen, and after that, then what? By this time, having had similar conversations with his brother, I'd gotten more practiced at my response. I'd talk about different religions, different beliefs: heaven, reincarnation, a return to the earth. I'd talk about how memory keeps people with us. How death is natural, that it doesn't hurt. How lots of people believe that we'll see our loved ones again after we die. How this is a question that humans have wrestled with ever since we became human, and people believe many, many different things. For a while, this largely sufficed. But one night when he was eight, during a particularly fraught bedtime conversation about mortality, he asked, "What do *you* believe?"

I took a breath. The room was dark. The dog snored at the foot of the bed. What did I believe? My son waited. Finally, finally, I said what felt truest. I told him that I don't know for sure—that no one does—but that I believe that love is permanent. That even after we die, our love is there; it never leaves.

My son wasn't comforted. I'd solved nothing, fixed nothing, promised nothing, explained nothing. But I felt calmer in that moment, more peaceful than I usually felt after pinging through a catalog of possibilities hoping to find the one that would take care of the problem.

Because how could anything take care of the problem? It's utterly incomprehensible: we're going to die, and so will everyone we love. I once read, I forget where, that humans are the only animals that know we're going to die. This may not be true—lots of animals demonstrate an awareness of death, and anyway, how do we know what any animal thinks?—but when I considered what it means to hold that awareness, I was willing to cut myself a break. How in the world are we supposed to go about the minutiae of our daily lives—slicing oranges, getting our teeth cleaned, sending emails—knowing that it will end, all

of it, for all of us? It's incredible what we carry every day, sometimes without even thinking about it. Like hauling a Buick on our backs without ever mentioning that it's there.

What I was saying to my son in that moment was: *I'll never leave*. And also, *I'll leave, of course, because we all will*. And also, *But I'll never leave*. This is the impossible paradox of loving someone. This is the impossible paradox we're all carrying, every moment of every day.

It helps me to remember that there is no perfect response, simultaneously honest and wonderfully reassuring, to offer a child saying *When I'm dead, I'll never see you again*.

Recently, recovering from COVID and needing a distraction, I started rewatching the TV show *The Good Place*. In one episode, Eleanor, a human, is trying to explain to the nonhuman Michael what it's like to be a person. Michael, utterly flummoxed by how humans can do anything at all knowing that their lives will inevitably end, is mid-breakdown over this fact, when Eleanor says matter-of-factly, "So we're all a little bit sad all the time. That's just the deal."

The first time I heard those lines, watching TV with my husband a couple of years before the pandemic would begin, I thought, *My god, that's it, that's being human*. The second time I heard them, in bed with my Gatorade and Advil on the bedside table, tired but fine, thanks to vaccines and science and luck and the fact that I'd been able to skirt the illness until it found its most recent milder iteration, it was a reminder that this isn't one

person's problem, or one day's problem, but everyone's, all the time, this impossible daily reckoning. The truth of that was a balm. The truth of how hard it is, and how we're all in it together.

When my son, who simply hadn't quite learned how jokes worked yet (it would be years before either kid would learn not to start *all* jokes with "knock knock," regardless of whether "who's there" was meant to follow), told his horsey joke, my laughter was real. The joke was so funny in its absurdity, and simultaneously so exactly right. The horse was running out of time. Aren't we all? All of us, a little bit sad all the time, doing our awkward best to comfort and be truthful, to say the almost-right thing, setting the alarm, waking up, making coffee as the sky begins to soften into morning, laughing at jokes because they don't make sense, and because, my god, they do, every day these tiny and monumental moments, all these impossibilities that add up to a life.

Perfect Sentence

7:00 A.M.

"HOW DO YOU SPELL 'CLOUDS FOLDED OVER THEM'?" asked my son. I was sweeping up the breakfast crumb mess, and he was sitting at the table, writing a story in his large white sketchbook. At six, our oldest was a precocious reader if not yet an expert speller, and had recently become interested in writing his own stories. Consequently, I had gotten very good at absently spelling words (*forest, lightning bolt, dragon*) while sweeping or paying bills or returning student emails. My sister-in-law, a pediatrician, once described our oldest as "kinetic," which I understood to be synonymous with "never again will you do a crossword puzzle on a Sunday," so when these rare moments of stillness happened, I seized them, tried to squash three hours' worth of things-to-be-done into ten minutes.

Then: "How do you spell 'clouds folded over them'?" he said.

"What?" I said, not sure I'd heard right.

My son repeated his question.

I repeated mine.

My son laughed like I was joking. "'*Clouds folded over them!*'" he said. "How do you spell that?"

What I wasn't trying to do in those short spaces of quiet was read or write. As a poet, I'd been stuck for months, bogged down in my own brain, resenting my poems for cycling again and again over the same territory. I'd open files and shut them. I'd type a line and delete it. And as a reader, I'd stalled out. I'd purchase new books—with beautiful matte covers, with perfect serif fonts, full of poems or stories or essays I knew I'd love—and stack them neatly on the ottoman. I wasn't opening them. I was reading the blurbs, maybe the dedication, and then setting them aside for Later. I couldn't access written language—there was too much of it. Too many good books to read any of them; too many good poems already out there to try to add any of my own. It felt like bobbing for apples if the apples had been replaced with planets. My teeth couldn't find purchase on something so massive.

But *clouds folded over them. Folded over.* The people were standing there in the field, and *clouds folded over them.* I could picture it, could picture the movement of the sky, the shift of the light. The word *folded* sparked inside me. *Over. Clouds.* It was a perfect sentence. Even better, it was one perfect sentence. Just one.

I thought about that one perfect sentence as I swept the crumbs into the dustpan. I said it out loud before bed. I put it in my pocket. I held it in my mouth. I folded it over me and went out into the world, where, I remembered now, there were forests, and lightning bolts, and dragons.

Parenting Metaphor

8:00 A.M.

THE MORNING HAS BEEN THE USUAL CHAOS OF toothbrushing negotiations and frantic sock searches, plus I discovered upon opening the freezer that we were out of the cinnamon Eggo French toast sticks, which caused a brief but passionate mutiny from both kids. My husband whipped up the world's fastest pancakes while I scrambled to make sure the big one's library book and hoodie were in his bookbag, the little one had his bag of *M* words for Alphabet Day (magnet, stuffed monkey, plastic muffin, vaguely grumpy-looking toy octopus I decided was mad), water bottles at the ready for both. Finally, finally, everyone was out the door, my husband and oldest in one car, on their way to first grade drop-off, the little one and I heading to preschool.

Now we're in the car, and I take a breath, let it out slowly. We've done it, again. Every morning this gauntlet of pandemonium, this scrambling that somehow catches us off guard every time. Why didn't I make sure the socks were neatly paired? Why did I neglect to check the freezer before doing yesterday's grocery shopping? Why, why did I wait until this morning to gather the *M* words?

But I know why—because I was doing something else. Because I was folding towels instead of pairing socks. I was playing Battleship instead of checking the freezer. I was watching a TV show about zombies with my husband instead of gathering *M* objects. And because I've learned that it wouldn't matter how much I prepared, not really, because there would be some other twist I hadn't seen coming. We'd have the Eggos but this would be the day someone decided never to eat Eggos again. I'd have the socks ready but one shoe would have vanished into the ether.

Now, though, I'm in the car, and I'm driving, and my son is safely buckled into his car seat behind me. He's wearing socks and shoes, his teeth are brushed, his *M* bag is next to him. I allow myself a moment of relief—for this moment, I've got it handled.

From the back seat, the little one says, "Mommy, can you hold this?" and I reach back. He often hands me his water bottle when he's done with it so I can put it in the cupholder next to me, and I'm ready for the cool cylinder in my hand.

What I feel instead is small, hard, sharp. I glance down.

I'm holding a horseshoe crab claw.

I have no idea where he got it; my kids collect beach treasures, but we haven't been near the ocean for months and months. I've been in the back seat every day, buckling car seats, searching for missing books and toys, and have never come across the claw. I feel a momentary thrill, like when a roller coaster crests the top of a hill and you realize suddenly that right now, in this moment, everything is beyond your control. "Thank you," I say.

"You're welcome," says my son.

Truth

9:00 A.M.

I'D TAKEN THE LITTLE ONE GROCERY SHOPPING, and on our way out, on a whim, we'd bought a bouquet of orange tulips. At home, he helped me strip off the extra leaves and place the flowers carefully in our red vase.

A few mornings later, he was sitting on my lap, looking at the tulips. It was a Saturday; we'd just finished breakfast and had nowhere to be. My oldest and his dad were playing basketball outside, and for a while the little one and I listened to the steady thump-thump of the ball on the driveway. Then he turned to me and asked, "Are these flowers going to turn into apples?"

I paused. I wanted so badly to say "maybe." I wanted to let him think that a tulip might turn into an apple, or a maple leaf into a gecko, or any small beautiful thing into another small beautiful thing. But I didn't want to lie, and so I said, gently, "No, they'll stay flowers."

"How do you know that?" he asked. He wasn't challenging me or being rude. He was asking. How did I *know,* how did I *absolutely know* the tulips wouldn't turn into apples?

And how did I? It's true I'd never seen it happen, never heard of it happening. It's true there's no scientific evidence that tulips-into-apples is a possibility. But it's also true that a fire has been burning below the ground in a Pennsylvania town since 1962. It's true that there's a forest in Brazil where mushrooms glow bright green at night. Lake Hillier in Western Australia is pink as bubblegum. The horned lizard shoots toxic blood from its eyes when threatened—not just a little bit, but an impressive arc, a stream. My children were once clusters of cells, were once little aquatic creatures inside my own body. None of this should be real. I know less than one trillionth of what there is to know about the world. I understand even less than that. Still, my job as a parent is to teach, to prepare my children for what it means to live in the world, to try to share the truth as I know it.

My son was looking at me, waiting for my answer. How *did* I know? It had rained last night, and through the window, the wet leaves of the holly gleamed like emeralds in the morning sun. "I just do," I said, and my stomach twinged a bit as I heard the lie leave my mouth.

What It Sounds Like

10:00 A.M.

BEFORE I HAD A CHILD, I'D HEARD PLENTY ABOUT how a mother's devotion to her kids is primal. And I got it. I could imagine that sort of wild, beyond the brain love, the kind of protectiveness that can sprout claws and incisors. I expected having a child to change my priorities, my routines, my capacity for tenderness and rage.

I didn't expect it to change my soundscape.

But my son's cries were lava. They were lightning. They were a hot razor raked through my insides. The instant I heard them, my milk would start flowing—my body's way of saying, before my brain could get there, *Here, let me fix it.*

In his book *Silence: In the Age of Noise,* the explorer Erling Kagge writes that silence can be found within, even in the noisiest of circumstances. It is, he explains, "more of an idea. A notion."

Either this is bullshit, or I'm doing it wrong.

Summer 2018: the news about the Honduran woman whose breastfeeding infant was taken from her by federal authorities. This story was the flashing red light at the top of a mounting skyscraper of inconceivable reports: Children separated from their parents at the border. Children kept in cages at "facilities." Parents told that their children were going to bathe, guards saying they were "following orders"—unmistakable echoes of another horror.

Homeland Security officials denied they'd removed any breastfeeding infants.

Natalia Cornelio, the criminal justice director for the Texas Civil Rights Project, said, "I know what I heard from this lady. She told it to me in tears."

I thought for a long time about what this mother might have heard as her child was carried away. About what those sounds did to her body.

Sometimes my son would cry when he wasn't hungry or wet or tired. He would cry just because he was a new human—and he was mysterious. The wailing would go on and on, rattling through me as I tried everything I could to fix it.

But sometimes I couldn't fix it. And sometimes when I couldn't, I'd hand our son over to my husband and shut myself in our bathroom, turn on the fan, stand there under its loud hum. The relief was immediate: as soon as I blocked out the crying, my breathing returned to normal, my lava-blood cooled. I'd stand there inside the blessed white noise for a few minutes, then return to where my husband was doing his own unsuccessful best. Our son would still be wailing. "Okay," I'd say and reach for him again.

In grad school my friend and her partner had a baby. We were all young, and parties were weekly, but I marveled when my friend told a handful of us to come over on Saturday and bring some wine. Their child was maybe two months old. I'd always imagined one's life pausing once a baby was born, rotating in place, suspended, like some sort of orb in a '70s sci-fi movie, and then returning to earth completely transformed. What did I know? I was years from having kids myself.

When I showed up, the gathering was in full swing. Not a party, exactly, but a small group of twenty- and thirtysomethings hanging out, drinking, laughing. It wasn't quiet. "Where's the baby?" I asked my friend, wondering if maybe a grandparent had him for the weekend.

"He's asleep in there," she replied, nodding toward a slightly ajar bedroom door a yard from where we were standing.

I was aghast. "Aren't you worried we're going to wake him up?"

"Nah," she said, "we want him to get used to noise. Otherwise we'll have to be quiet all the time." She laughed and turned to greet another guest. *What a genius plan*, I thought.

For the first two days of our oldest son's life, he slept almost constantly—a peaceful, cozying-in slumber. *This is bliss*, I thought, gazing at his impossibly perfect ears. Then he stopped sleeping altogether. Or, more accurately, he stopped sleeping for any substantial stretch. Twenty minutes at a time for a nap, maybe an hour and fifteen minutes at night. We tried the rocking, the swaddle, the *shush*ing, the ocean noise, the swinging. None of it worked. He would fall asleep only after nursing and would wake the second I laid him down. My husband said, not really joking, that someone could make millions inventing a long-handled tray to slide infants into bed without disturbing them—a baby pizza peel. I developed a technique: I'd lay my son down and keep my hands on him. I'd count to five and remove one finger. Count to five again and remove another. I'd do this until I'd slowly detached myself from him. Sometimes it worked. Other times his gray-blue eyes would pop open, and again I'd rock him, *shush* him, swing him, sing to him, reswaddle, reswaddle, reswaddle.

For months I was bleary with lack of sleep. My days were fogged. I felt vaguely disassembled, as if each of my atoms had a teeny bit of extra space around it. It was like being slightly drunk all the time, which isn't a feeling you want unless you've been drinking. So whenever our son did nod off during the night, I dove for sleep myself like a hawk for a rabbit. I was ravenous, single-minded, unabashedly greedy. I was absolutely desperate not to wake my son, desperate for the quiet that might let his sleep continue.

I became silence obsessed; I'd do anything to create and preserve it. If I wanted a snack before bed, I'd find something that didn't require unwrapping or utensil clinking. If I got up in the night to pee, I wouldn't flush the toilet. If I had to sneeze while in bed, I'd bury my face in my pillow, swallow the sneeze so that my throat stung. A car horn outside, an incoming text, a cat fight across the street made my heart spasm in an illogical concord of panic and rage—*Shut up,* I thought fervently, *shut up.* Our bed creaked, so I'd find one position for sleep and hold myself to it all night.

According to the Department of Homeland Security, in the six weeks between April 19 and May 31, 2018, nearly two thousand minors were separated from adults at the US–Mexico border. When questioned about the cruelty of this policy, the attorney general said, "I would cite you to the Apostle Paul and his clear and wise command in Romans 13, to obey the laws of the government because God has ordained them for the purpose of order." I read this quote online. I couldn't bear to watch the clip because I didn't want to hear his voice.

The first time I spent a night away from my son was a year and a week after his birth. He'd stopped nursing a few days before, and though I was sad to be at the end of that deep and still intimacy, I was glad to have some measure of freedom again. So when my friend invited me up to spend a night with her in Brooklyn while we were in New Jersey with family, I packed a bag and left my son and husband. On the train from Little Silver to Penn Station I read an entire book of poetry I'd been meaning to check out for more than a year. I talked to my sister. I watched from the window as we passed sub shops and billboards and marshes. All through the train ride I felt the miles between my son and me increasing. It was a thrill. It was a wound.

In New York my friend and I went to an excellent Italian restaurant where I drank wine and ate affogato for dessert and was exquisitely aware of not worrying about either the alcohol or the caffeine. We stayed up for a bit, talking, and then I stretched out on the air mattress in her living room, read a magazine—luxuriating in staying up late because I was guaranteed not to be needed—and fell asleep, exhilarated and exhausted.

Just after midnight I woke with a start. My son was crying. I sat up, heart racing, fumbled for my glasses, realized they weren't on the bedside table, realized there was no bedside table, realized I was fifty miles away from him. My heart slowed. I listened. There were city sounds outside—people laughing, a bottle breaking—but no babies crying. I lay back down. Two more times that night I woke in the same way, having invented sound where it wasn't. My body no longer knew any other way to sleep.

When our oldest was two and our youngest hadn't yet been born, we spent the winter holidays at my mother's house in Pennsylvania. On New Year's Eve, after carefully, painstakingly getting our son down to sleep in our upstairs room, my husband and I poured glasses of champagne. My sister and brother-in-law, sharing a room downstairs with their four-month-old son, apologized in advance for the crying we were sure to hear during the night. *No worries, it isn't a problem at all,* we said, and we meant it. Around one in the morning, our own son still sleeping peacefully in his crib at the foot of our bed, we heard our nephew start his fussing. "Not our kid," I whispered to my husband, and we high-fived silently in the dark and went back to our dreams.

While my sons watch a cartoon about an environmentalist cat, I check the news and learn the US government has opened so-called tender-age shelters for babies and young children who have been forcibly separated from their parents at the border. Reports from inside these shelters describe rooms full of preschool-age kids sobbing without ceasing.

Imagine being the mother of one of these tender-age children imagining what that sounds like.

I elected to have an epidural with each of my sons' births. The first went perfectly. The second seemed to have gone perfectly. Then, sometime the next day, my head began to ache. I told the attending OB, who dismissed my concerns. The epidural had gone smoothly, so this was, he insisted, just a postpartum wrinkle. But the headache got worse in the days after I went home. When I sat up or stood, the pain was excruciating; when I lay flat on my back, the pain ebbed. These symptoms precisely matched the description of a spinal headache, caused when the epidural needle punctures the dura mater that protects the spinal cord. Spinal fluid leaks through this puncture, which decreases the pressure—the cushioning—of the cerebrospinal fluid around the brain. I made an appointment at the women's clinic, where I saw the doctor who had performed the epidural and told her I was worried I might have a spinal headache. No, she said, and she too told me that because everything had gone well, this was just a bad headache, probably a migraine caused by hormones.

"But I've never had a migraine," I said.

"Birth does strange things to a woman's body," she said, and sent me home.

On the seventh day I woke with double vision. I looked at the house across the street and couldn't count the windows. My baby's face swam. I began to panic. The whole world was physically shifting around me. My head hurt and hurt and hurt. I called the clinic again and told them I was coming back.

In the office the nurse secured the cuff around my arm and stepped back to monitor. "Wow," she said after a minute. "Do you normally have high blood pressure?"

"No," I said.

"Wow," she said again.

The doctor—the same one who had sent me away with a migraine diagnosis—listened to my symptoms again and then said, as if the idea were just occurring to her, that it sounded like I might have a spinal headache. "Let's get you over to the hospital for a blood patch," she said and smiled, glad to have solved my problem.

A blood patch is, essentially, a second epidural, only instead of injecting anesthesia, the doctor injects a patient's own blood, pumped directly from the patient's arm to the hole in her spine. That blood clots and seals the hole, effectively "patching" it and stopping the leak. For people like me—people terrified of hospitals, people who have to shove down every fear and instinct in order to have a child in the first place—this is borderline nightmare territory.

In the hospital I was wheeled to a recovery area near the OR, which felt like a weird white dreamscape: twenty or thirty or fifty (with my doubled vision I could take in only impressions) tiny "rooms," each with a bed and not much else, separated only by white curtains, no walls. I was shifted from the gurney to the bed and left alone. They were fitting me between scheduled surgeries and true emergencies, so I had a long time to lie flat on the white sheets, eyes closed against the overhead lights, and listen.

At first there wasn't much to hear—someone wheeling a rattling cart, two nurses hashing out their lunch order. Then the crying started. It was a child, and the crying was continuous and heartbreaking and vastly, vastly sad. It wasn't a wail of sudden pain, like from getting a shot. It wasn't even very loud. It was just steady. It did not stop. I didn't hear anyone talking to the child, and the child didn't say any words. There was just the crying.

I didn't know anything about the child: how old he was, why he was there, what had prompted his tears. But he sounded familiar to me. Specifically, he sounded like my three-year-old son, and I couldn't help him. It hurt more than the headache, more than the needle in my spine was about to. I felt it with an intensity that shocked me, even in my addled state. Deep down, lightning in the veins. *Someone go help that child,* I thought, but there was no one for me to address. I was scared, waiting alone for the doctor in that weird white space, thinking about the leak in my spinal cord, thinking about the needles to come. And if I was that scared—a thirty-five-year-old woman, a grown-up who understood fully the mechanism of this treatment, the very limited actual threat the procedure posed—how terrified must that child have been of whatever was about to happen or already had? Where were his parents? The doctors, the nurses? Why was no one with him?

Finally a doctor whisked into my makeshift room. She checked my vitals: my blood pressure was still alarmingly high, my heart was racing, and I'm sure my eyes were alien-wide in that way my husband has told me they get when I'm worried. "You're very upset," she said brusquely, "and you need to calm down. You're making it worse for yourself. I can't do this until you relax." And because I had to get this fixed—because I couldn't sit up, because I couldn't see, because I had to get back to my infant who was hungry, because my three-year-old might need me—I did. I breathed. I willed my heart to slow, my eyes to look human. I concentrated hard on pulling myself the fuck together. "Okay," I said to the doctor after a few minutes, and she set about hooking me up to the complicated network of needles and tubes that would repair me.

It wasn't until much later—after I was home, recovering, vision still doubled but headache receding, nursing one son while listening to the other play with his grandmother—that I realized I hadn't heard the crying child again after the doctor came in. Maybe he had stopped crying or was moved somewhere else. More likely, I tuned him out. I had my own children to get back to, and I could do that only if I shut out the world enough to calm down, so I did. I'm ashamed to say I didn't ask about the child, didn't look for him as I was wheeled out on another gurney after the needles and tubes had done their job. Out of earshot, out of mind. Or, more accurately: out of mind, out of earshot.

Sometimes I still wonder what happened to that little boy.

What a luxury idle wondering is.

In the ProPublica audio file of detained minors, the crying of the children—ten of them—is steady, sustained, gutting. It's awful in a way that language can't quite describe. The *Washington Post* reported "a chorus of children sobbing and asking for their parents, some in what sounds like significant levels of distress." The *New York Times* wrote about "immigrant children calling out desperately for their parents after being separated from them by United States immigration authorities." I can get into specifics and subjective metaphor, can detail the catches of breath, the way *Mami* and *Papá* transform into much longer words inside the chaos of sobs. But none of this even gets close.

About one minute into the recording, a border patrol officer says, "Well, we have an orchestra here, right? What we're missing is a conductor." The man's voice doesn't seem cruel, and because I don't know much Spanish, and because things don't always sound like what they are, it's possible that if the recording didn't have subtitles, I'd have mistaken him for someone trying to comfort the children.

All parents have their own tended, unshakable fears. One might obsess about choking, another about drowning, another about car wrecks. As a mother of white sons, my compendium of reasonable fears is shorter than so many other mothers'. I worry about the cruelties of the world and how they might find my children, but I don't usually worry that my boys will be specifically targeted because of who they are. My most tenacious worry has been about what might happen during sleep, during those moments when I'm not right there. While my children were babies, I slipped into their rooms multiple times each night to watch their backs rising and falling in the night-light's glow. Now that my kids are older I check less frequently, but I still check. When I do, I rely on sound in their big-kid-dark bedrooms, putting my ear close to their faces and listening for the breath that lets me go to sleep myself.

In the press-conference video, the press secretary is fielding increasingly heated questions about the administration's zero-tolerance policy separating immigrant children from their families. Finally one reporter makes it personal. "You're a parent," he says to her. "Don't you have any empathy for what these people are going through?"

An admission: when I first saw the articles about the border separations in my news feed, when I began seeing my friends post and tweet about these horrors, I didn't click on any of the links. I didn't want to read the stories. I wanted the country on mute for a little while. I wanted a break from worry and wreckage. Like so many people living in the United States in 2018, I was exhausted. Worn down. I was having a nice summer—my oldest son learning to swim, my youngest developing a deep commitment to ice cream, my dreams having returned to standard bizarro dream fare after a spring spent working against a statewide campus-carry bill and dreaming nightly about guns—and I didn't want to give that up. So, for a couple of days, I let myself pretend it wasn't happening. I avoided Twitter. I skipped past NPR. I didn't acknowledge this to myself, exactly—I just carefully curated my world for a few days, which is one of the more obscene levels of privilege to which one can admit.

Not my kid.

But when the press conference appeared in my Facebook feed, having been shared by a handful of friends with comments like *infuriating* and *abominable* and *evil,* I heard what my cowardice had been saying. I watched the video—first with only subtitles, to ease myself in, and then, like a penance, with audio.

The press secretary tries to brush off the man asking the questions. Tries to open the floor to the next reporter, a woman from the *Washington Post*. On the subtitled version, the chaos of this scene isn't apparent, but with sound the press secretary's desperation is clear. "Go ahead," she says to the woman, talking over the man's questions. "Please," she says. "I want to recognize you. Go ahead."

But the man keeps going. "They come to the border with nothing and you throw children in cages. You're a parent," he says. "You're a parent of young children. Don't you have any empathy for what they go through?"

The press secretary keeps trying to get the next reporter to take the floor. But the next reporter doesn't speak, not yet. Instead, she waits. She lets the questions hover. Her silence makes room for them.

The last few years have been so endlessly tumultuous for our country and world that it's easy for that summer to feel like the distant past. I have to dig to track down updates about the children; when I do, I find the update from September 14, 2022, from the Biden administration's Interagency Task Force on the Reunification of Families. According to the report, 3,855 children were identified as having been separated. As of September 2022, the report notes, 886 had not had reunification confirmed or were listed as "status unknown," 191 were "in process," and 2,766 had been reunited with family.

"Reunited" sounds like a word that means *success*. But trauma's roots are deep, and they spread. Some young children didn't recognize their parents when they were returned to them.

Some believed they'd been intentionally abandoned. According to a study conducted by the not-for-profit NGO Physicians for Human Rights, "Parents reported severe residual effects of sustained trauma including physiological manifestations of anxiety and panic, experiencing 'pure agony,' emotional and mental despair, and suicidal thoughts." These families will carry the effects of that summer with them for the rest of their lives. These families are the success stories.

I'm on the beach with my husband and kids; it's midmorning, most of the long summer day still ahead of us. We've brought crackers and cherries and PB&J sandwiches that will soon be seasoned with sand. We've set up, as we always do, near a lifeguard stand, and my sons are digging just beyond the surf, working to create their own tide pool. It's easy for tragedy to feel far away here, the sky a brash blue, dolphins arcing by. The beach is loud in that beach way: the ocean's constant roar and rumble, seagulls shrieking, everywhere kids yelling and laughing and crying, Toto's "Rosanna" playing from someone's portable speakers. The waves are big today, strong, crashing hard against the shoreline.

Suddenly a lifeguard's whistle pierces through the sounds, and everything hushes except the ocean. The guard is standing, waving his red flags emphatically. I follow his gaze. The water is crowded: teenagers boogie-boarding, kids splashing, people bobbing out beyond the breakers. A man and woman are standing knee-deep in the surf, talking, a little girl on the man's shoulders.

Nearly everyone in the ocean—the teenagers, the bobbers, the kids—looks at the lifeguard. Having been in the ocean during plenty of lifeguard whistles myself, I know what they're thinking: maybe they've unwittingly broken some beach rule, gotten too far out, too reckless, too close to some unmarked shipwreck. Only the parents standing in the surf with the little girl don't turn toward the guard. How could it be them? They're just standing, chatting, in shallow water.

But it is them. When they finally turn toward the whistle that isn't stopping, the lifeguard signals again, and the father pauses for a moment, as if trying to make sense of something senseless. His daughter is safe. He has her, is holding her ankles securely, isn't going to drop her, would never drop her. His stillness as he looks at the lifeguard says *You don't understand, I'm not going to let her go*. But the lifeguard whistles again, gesturing, and his whistle says *Just because you'd never let her go doesn't mean the ocean won't take her*.

Carefully the father lifts the little girl off his shoulders. The guard sits back down, and the beach returns to its peaceful chaos: the kids, the crashing, the gulls, all the sounds we cling to, the ones that tell us everything is fine.

Naming

11:00 A.M.

AT THE TOP OF THE YELLOW CORKSCREW SLIDE, the little one, newly four, paused and looked down at me. "If you were a butterfly," he said, "what would you name you?"

I realized he must have been thinking about this question as he played, as he climbed the green metal steps to the slide's apex, as he looked down and saw me waiting for him at the bottom. On this April morning in Mississippi, I'd been thinking about some other questions, like *Why is it a million degrees before noon?*, and *What in the world are we going to do on weekends next month when the slides will be too hot to use?* But my son's question momentarily distracted me. What *would* I name the butterfly-me? Hazel? Ivy? Lover-of-Sweetness? It's always seemed to me that choosing one's own name must require the deepest level of self-knowing. Growing up, I felt more suited to my real name, Catherine, than to my bright-eyed nickname, Katie, though over time I settled into both and their contradictions. But if I could name myself? If I flew from bloom to bloom, if I had black-and-orange wings twice the size of my body, if I could choose what I'd answer to? Who would I be? Iridescence? Sun Wing? Soft-Wind-Against-the-Iris? Could I call myself One-Who-Delivers-Comfort? Could I still call myself Mother? I want to say, *I'll answer to whatever you call me.*

Before I had a baby, I wondered about nicknames. What would I casually call my first son when he was born? Was this something I should plan in advance? Shouldn't I have something prepared, some affectionate term at the ready? Every time I tried to think of something, I came up blank. Then there he was and the nicknames came fast and unsought, as if some secret faucet had been turned.

I've called my children *bear, buddy, sweetheart. Little one, big one, baby, dude, monkey, noodle, sweet potato pie*. I've called them *goofball* and *my love*. And they've answered.

"Wow," I said, trying to gather myself for some kind of response, "that's a really great question. I don't know, I'd have to think about—"

"Venom?" said my son, then disappeared into the slide's bright mouth.

Stings

12:00 P.M.

"WELL? HOW WAS IT?" MY MOTHER ASKED AS I stepped off the bus after my first day of kindergarten. Things had gone well. There was a sizable playground, and I'd learned we were going to watch caterpillars turn into butterflies. Before I could say any of this, a bee began buzzing around our bare legs. I'd never been stung, but I was no fool, and I looked at my mother in panic. "It's okay," she said. "Just stay still. If you don't bother it, it won't bother you."

I held still. And the bee stung my knee and I burst into wails and my poor mother carried me home and mixed up a paste of baking soda and water and applied it to the sting, and then spent the afternoon apologizing. "I'm so sorry, honey," she said. "I don't know why it did that." She'd tell the story again and again throughout my childhood. "She was so happy getting off the bus!" she'd say. It became part of family lore, one of those anecdotes that gets repeated to neighbors over backyard beers for laughs and commiseration. But her voice would tighten as she went on. "And I'd told her to stay still, and then this bee *stung her anyway*. It was her *first day of kindergarten*."

As I got older, she changed the words she used. "That asshole bee," she'd say, "I still can't believe it did that to you."

"It really was an asshole," I'd agree, and we'd sip our margaritas and laugh.

When my oldest son turned five, he developed a terror of bees. He hadn't been stung, but, like me, he was no fool. He had *The Big Book of Insects* and had heard stories from friends. He lived in mortal fear of his annual flu shot, so a bee sting seemed incomprehensibly awful. Mississippi springtime—lush, green, practically indecent with wisteria and dogwood—was dead to him. We tried coaxing, logic, peer pressure, bribes. Nothing would get him to agree to a game of Frisbee or a Saturday playground visit. And when we *were* outside and a bee buzzed by, he took off like lightning—just as fast, and just as zigzagging. The word that comes to mind is *crazed*, as in the every-which-way cracks on a ceramic glaze. He didn't look where he was going—he just ran. I was terrified he'd dash into the street in his panic, and after weeks of yelling after him to *stop running!*, one day I sat him down on the stump in our front yard. His eyes darted from crepe myrtle to crepe myrtle as I knelt to his level.

"Buddy," I said, "you can't just bolt off like that. I know bees are scary, but a bee sting is way better than getting hit by a car."

"I can't help it," said my son, and I knew he was being honest.

“I get it,” I said, “but the bees don’t *want* to sting you. They actually die if they do. They just want to get their nectar and keep their hive safe. Keep doing what you’re doing. You don’t need to run.” Then I heard myself say, “The thing about bees is, if you don’t bother them, they won’t bother you.”

Later that evening, while I cleared the dinner table and my sons laughed and bickered, I ran through justifications in my head. I try to be truthful with my kids, insofar as it isn’t cruel to do so. I want them to trust me, and I felt guilty about what I’d said. But I also want my kids to trust the world. So I told myself *it was mainly true,* and *there are exceptions to everything,* and *he can’t avoid the yard forever,* and *anyway, what else could I have done?*

Now my oldest, my bee fearer, is in middle school, and I can’t steward his world the way I could when he was five. We have rules and conversations about phones and YouTube, but his radius of exposure and understanding has widened exponentially. This means we get to have thoughtful, ranging talks about everything from climate change to Fortnite. It also means that he knows about the big news stories.

One night, when I went into his dark bedroom to say good night, he said, “What if a shooter comes to my school?” He wasn’t asking *what should I do*; he was asking the bigger, broader question—*What if this happens?*

I was glad for the dark as I fumbled for my answer. I told him that it’s extremely unlikely to happen, that the teachers know what to do and the school's resource officer is there to keep everyone safe. I did not lie. But I also chose not to offer practical advice—*silence your phone, play dead, cover yourself in someone else's blood*—because to do so would be to acknowledge the realness of this horror. I couldn't bear to make his fear spikier, more violent—not in that soft dark room, not before sleep, not with him right there next to me, his brother in the next room already dreaming. I spent the rest of the night worrying that I should have provided the practical advice.

If we're looking for metaphors, a mother is not a queen bee but a worker. She tends and carries. She disposes and guards. Unlike the queen, her stinger, when she needs it, is barbed.

My mother's sharpest anger is reserved for those who have hurt her children: the pretty first grade teacher whose cruelty nearly put me off school forever, the boy who shattered my sister's bus window with a BB gun, leaving her unharmed but afraid. Bring up one of these people even now, and my mother's voice hardens into an iron rod. A kind, hilarious person, she will not waste forgiveness on them. And I know that she has not forgiven the bee. We joke about it, but I know that even as she carried me home that day, soothed the sting with the paste she'd mixed, sat with me on the couch and made me laugh through the subsiding burning, even then—she was livid. She didn't show it, but her rage was humming through her veins: at this bee that had hurt her daughter, at the natural world that had no sense of honor. Fear isn't rational. Neither is anger. The bee had made a liar out of my mother, when all she'd tried to do was keep her kid safe.

When I was a child petrified by shots, my mother would say, "If I could take it for you, I would." Sometimes she would hold out her arm and ask the nurse to stick her instead—mainly joking but, I think, a tiny bit hoping that maybe, somehow, she'd be allowed to spare her children the needle's prick. When I was twenty-two and hysterical with fever and struggling through a serious bout of depression and anxiety, she said, "Honey, if I could take this for you, I would." When I was thirty-five and six days postpartum and terrified by my worsening headache and sudden double vision from a spinal fluid leak, my mother held a washcloth to my forehead, darkened the room, carried the baby to me when he needed to nurse, took him when he was done. I knew she would have taken my skull's throbbing, too, and my misery over being unable to sit up or focus on my son's face. She couldn't, of course, but she would have. She would have taken that bee sting gladly.

By the time my oldest was seven, he wasn't completely terrified of bees anymore. He didn't like them, and he still moved quickly to the other side of the yard when one buzzed near, but he'd learned that he had to shove the fear down in order to play a game of H-O-R-S-E or climb the crepe myrtle. In late spring that year, though, in the middle of the night he started occasionally appearing next to my side of the bed and telling me there was a bee in his room.

The first time this happened, I was up like a flash, switching on lights, turning off the noise machine, listening. There was nothing. The second time I was a little slower to start my hunt. By the third time in two weeks, I said, "Honey, this is a dream you're having. There's nothing there." Even in the dark, I could see him struggling with himself. He wanted to believe me—but he thought he'd seen a bee. His fear had manufactured something nearly tangible out of his dreams. And I understand intimately that in the battle between fear and fact, sometimes fact gets walloped. So I walked him back to his room. I made a show of checking under his bed, in his closet, behind the dresser. I sat on his floor until he fell asleep.

He was four the day a text had come through from my university's emergency alert system saying there was an active shooter on campus. I was working in my office, and my first thought, once I could think, was *of course*. Before those words came, there was only a wordless flood of silent panic. Heart, stomach, hands shaking like jackhammers. My next thought was of my sons and how I would do literally anything to get home to them. Somehow I locked my door, crawled under my desk, silenced my phone. Then I stopped thinking about my children. My body wouldn't let me. *Stay sharp,* it said, *you cannot spare any emotion now*. In the dark under my desk, I felt steely, a rigid metal girder that would not break or bend.

It turned out there was no shooter. There were threats, misinformation, reasonable panic. It was a game of grown-up telephone. But for thirty-seven minutes it was real. My body told me so. When word finally went out that it had been a false alarm, I left immediately, grateful not to have any afternoon classes that day, desperate to have my sons in my car, in our house. My oldest son's preschool was on campus—a good mile from where the alleged shooter had been, but the preschool, like the rest of campus, had entered lockdown immediately, turned off lights, gotten everyone away from windows. When I picked him up that day, his teacher showed me a painting he'd made just after the all clear went out—fat red and black strokes across the large page, no form, just color and the force that clearly went into the painting. *It was an intense day for the kids,* she said. *They knew something was up.*

My youngest son was in daycare at a local church, and when I arrived to get him, he and his toddler classmates were in the small gated playground, scooting around on plastic three-wheelers, clambering into the playhouse, blowing bubbles. My son's teacher waved and came over, another child on her hip. *We were on lockdown so we just got outside a few minutes ago,* she said matter-of-factly, as if explaining a simple schedule change.

This is the part I haven't talked much about to anyone, because it's strange and ugly and not suited for anecdote. But that morning, crouched under my desk, my hands had eventually stopped shaking. My breathing gradually slowed. My body kept vigil while something happened. An unfolding, or a sort of birth. And when I crawled out from under my desk, there was a new animal inside me. A rage animal. It stayed there after the all clear came through. Its hackles raised at the daycare teacher's matter-of-factness, at the painting my son felt moved to make. When I read about Uvalde, and Parkland, and Sutherland Springs, and Las Vegas, and Orlando, and Kalamazoo, and San Bernardino, and Charleston, it swelled and pushed its spine against my own. Its anger is towering, bigger and taller than any I've known before. It's absurd, impossible, that this is happening and I can't stop it. That those who can won't. I try to walk next to this animal. I try to hide it from my sons. This animal's teeth are mine. It's made of blood and bone like everyone else, and it can't keep anyone safe. What good is an animal like that?

The spring my son started imagining bees in his room at night, I volunteered to chaperone his class field trip to the university entomological museum; I hoped the visit might help to quiet his worry. At the museum, his classmates were as hilariously inquisitive as you might expect (when one of the entomologists, a young guy with a twirled and waxed mustache, was showing the display case of blue morpho butterflies, one student raised his hand and asked, "Is that a bug in your ear?" "No," replied the entomologist, "it's a piercing."), and my son held a millipede, and I got to let a giant tarantula named the Ambassador crawl around the small bowl of my hands. Finally our group reached the last station: a live bee colony encased in glass, buzzing and humming. The scientist leading this part of the tour was also their beekeeper, and he showed us a picture of himself bearded in what looked like half the colony. He explained about the queen, about workers and drones, and then said, "Do you know what to do if a bee comes after you?"

One boy raised his hand. "Stand still," he said. He was solemn and confident, probably echoing his mother's advice.

The beekeeper's eyebrows arched in alarm. "Oh, no," he said, "that's the worst thing you can do. If a bee comes after you, you get out of there. Just get away. Just run."

My son, bless him, kept watching the bees and did not turn to look at me.

A few weeks after that field trip, I had the house to myself for the day. The kids were at school, my husband was teaching, and I'd spent the morning grading and responding to emails. At noon I shifted over into household tasks for a little while; not the most exciting break but pleasant enough, this work that didn't require much of my focus. In my mind I ran through tomorrow's class on line breaks as I carried the empty laundry basket down the hall to gather a load of dirty clothes. Did I have enough dry erase markers for my students to write on the whiteboards? Had I already uploaded that document, or no? As I passed my son's room, I heard a faint sound. It barely registered. It pinged the periphery of my brain, and I ignored it.

A few minutes later, as I walked back by his room with a basket of towels, I heard it again, still faint, still barely a sound at all. I kept walking for a few steps. Then I set down the laundry basket and backtracked. I peered into my son's room. My eyes landed on his closed blinds and somehow—I'll never know how—I spied a tiny black thread waving out from between them. I crept closer. The thread was a wasp's back leg. The wasp buzzed angrily against the blinds, trapped between them and the bright afternoon it could see but not reach. I snatched up a paperback and, quick as a cobra, yanked the cord that zipped the blinds upward. The wasp buzzed even more frantically and I whacked it. It was a big wasp, and my aim was poor, and I whacked it again and again. "Don't you fucking think about it," I hissed over and over like a madwoman.

When I see a spider in the house, I trap it under a cup and deliver it to the bushes outside. I do the same with lizards, ladybugs, beetles. I kill ants, but I feel bad about it, and sometimes I whisper an apology. It's true that a wasp's attack can be even more painful than a bee's, because wasps sting repeatedly without dying. It's true, too, that they tend to be aggressive. It was reasonable for me to kill the wasp. What wasn't reasonable was the ferocity with which I went about it. But I was angry, so angry. I was livid.

What I was saying as I swore at the wasp, as I smashed it over and over—against the window, then the windowsill, then the carpet where it twitched—was *Don't you dare hurt my child.* What I was saying was, *Oh my god, was there a wasp in his room all along?* What I was saying was, *Forgive me the lies I didn't mean as lies.* And then I killed that wasp. It was something I could do, and I did it.

A Total Solar Eclipse Is Visible from Any Given Point on Earth Once Every 375 Years, on Average

1:00 P.M.

FOR WEEKS WE'D BUILT UP THE ECLIPSE—HOW the moon would slowly creep in front of the sun until all that was left was a sliver, how it would feel like evening right in the middle of the afternoon. How unusual it was, how special, and how amazing that we happened to live in a place where we'd have such a perfect view. In our town, we were supposed to reach almost complete totality.

At 1:00 P.M., we picked the kids up early from school and headed to the campus lake. It was overcast, and I was worried—what if we couldn't see the eclipse at all, what if we'd built this up and then had only cloud cover to show for it? Maximum eclipse time for us would be 1:27 P.M., so the pressure was on. But as we pulled into the lake's parking lot, the clouds cleared and there, right above us, was the strange partial sun.

I handed out the special sunglasses to my husband and kids, put on my own, and gazed around the entire scene, taking in the change of light, of color, of atmosphere. The lake was still the lake, the sky was still the sky, but . . . different. As if someone had put a blue filter over everything. As if we were in a stylized film, or a dream. I was mesmerized by it all, by the way that this place I knew so well—this small lake whose perimeter track I walked every morning after dropping my children off at school and daycare—was suddenly otherworldly. Magic. Overhead, the sun was vanishing steadily, with razor precision. It had all worked: we'd gotten here. Our kids would have this memory.

Then my youngest son called out, breaking through my dream. "Look!" he yelled. "Look at this—it's *amazing*!" He was peering through the rails of the safety fence into the lake, where a handful of fish were swimming. They were smallish fish, the kind of fish unfortunately named *crappie*. They were always there; I saw them every morning.

But my son, three, had never seen them. "It's amazing," he said again, his back to the disappearing sun, as the shimmering fish sparked and swam beneath us.

Beachcombing

2:00 P.M.

IT WAS A BRIGHT, HOT JULY AFTERNOON. THE SUN was spangling the ocean; blue rental umbrellas covered the shoreline. We'd eaten the peanut butter crackers and Goldfish, we'd made drip castles, we'd dug for sand crabs, those shiny, cicada-sized creatures that burrow just below the sand where the tide comes in. My husband and oldest son were back in the water for the fourth time, and the little one's good humor was beginning to wear thin.

"Let's find the prettiest shell and put it in here," I said, holding up a red plastic bucket. When I was a child, I'd been an expert shell collector. I could occupy hours searching for the perfect, unbroken scallops, the gleaming mussels, the snaking, parchment-brown casings that held hundreds of miniature whelks. I filled bowls with the shells; I decorated my dresser with them; with my mother's help, I glued them onto delicate wooden boxes as homemade Christmas gifts. Briefly I thought of how later that day I could run out to the craft store and buy a glue gun.

"Okay," said my son agreeably. He reached down and picked up the white innards of a dead sand crab. He placed them carefully in the bucket.

Carousel

3:00 P.M.

SO YOU'RE RIDING THE BOARDWALK CAROUSEL with your son and everything is so loud and the old calliope song is blaring but in a friendly way and you're going around and around and as you pass the Frog Bog game the stuffed stingrays are so purple and the ocean is *right there* glinting and crashing and there are so many people on vacation, sunburn striped below their eyes, everyone's shoulders and ankles sandy, kids crying and pulling on hands and eating ice cream that's melting just everywhere and you're about to slip down the reverie slide into a brief reflection on impermanence and mortality and This Very Moment and then your son says, "Oh! We need to get another goody bag at the library!" and he means another raffle ticket, he and his brother have been doing the summer reading program and they've both just banked another ten hours, which unlocks the next badge and the next raffle ticket, so he's concerned, and you say, "Don't worry, we will," and you will, and how dare you step outside this moment to consider this moment, look at your son, your lacquered horse he named Sparkly, look at how this moment is right here, and now it isn't, and now, blessedly, another moment is.

One Man's Treasure Is Another Man's Treasure

4:00 P.M.

IT HAD BEEN A GOOD DAY AT THE STATE PARK, IF A long one: a picnic, some makeshift Frisbee golf (*Okay,* said my husband, *see if you can hit that big tree in three throws*), some tadpole discovery, some playground acrobatics. There had also been some minor knee scraping and wailing, and my husband and I had worked hard, because the kids rarely wanted to do the same thing at the same time and they were both still young enough to need unflagging supervision. When one wanted to explore the lakeshore, the other wanted to climb on the playground; when one wanted to look for four-leaf clovers, the other wanted to play tag. But we made it work, and we had a good time.

Now, though, we were all back in the car, facing the forty-five-minute drive home. The kids were sweaty and hot and tired; our picnic lunch had been a long time ago. As we pulled onto the highway, they began sniping at each other in the back seat. *I want that book! No, I had it first! Give it to me! No! Hey! Mommmmm!*

I felt my impatience rising. I took a breath and closed my eyes. I knew that sweaty and hot and tired and hungry equaled tears. But I was *also* sweaty and hot and tired and hungry, and doing my best not to slip over into my own meltdown. *Why is it so hard to make everyone happy?* I thought. Then—

"Look!" cried the three-year-old. "Flowers!"

"Look!" cried the six-year-old. "A cemetery!"

They were both so pleased with what they'd spotted, and their joy was a balm. For a moment the air inside the car shimmered with silence, with the unexpected relief of both boys, these two very different humans, finding, simultaneously, sights that delighted them. It was only when I turned around to follow their pointing fingers that I realized they were looking at the same thing.

Resolution

5:00 P.M.

"IT'S EXACTLY A YEAR!" EXCLAIMED MY OLDEST, seven, from the back seat.

"What is? A year since what?" I said, turning down the radio.

"Since this exact moment!" he replied. He must have seen my confusion, because he went on: "Every second is a year from something. Why can't we just say 'Happy New Year' all the time?"

Resolution: *the action or (in later use esp.) an act of resolving or determining; something which has been resolved upon; a fixed or positive intention.*

On New Year's Eve a couple of months earlier, we'd let the kids stay up later than usual, snacking on cheese and crackers and chocolate. We'd read them their stories, kissed them good night, said "See you next year." The air felt like snow. There were winter stars and I wore new flannel pajamas. My husband and I drank a little wine, ate Japanese takeout, went to bed well before midnight. All night, I was electric with gratitude. Everything felt *right,* like great silver bells ringing in harmony.

Some days I watch myself being the mother I imagined I might be: firm but never ruffled, doling out special holiday snacks, laughing as the kids pillage couches for fort pillows or pile their toys to make an offering to the daddy longlegs in the corner. Some days I look at myself right there in the thick of motherhood and think, *Well done.* I post on Facebook on those days; I send goofy family pictures to my parents, my sister. Everything feels balanced.

But some days my fuse is shorter. Some days I raise my voice to say *I shouldn't have to ask about socks four times!* Some days I turn my back to unload the dishwasher and instantly someone is yelling and someone is crying and *Guys, I have to be able to leave you alone for two minutes!* I've threatened to pull the car over. I've pulled the car over. I've closed books much too hard. I've slammed the cupboard door because the dinnertime howling has reached a fever pitch and *Fine, buddy, here's the applesauce!*

"Temper" means *to mix correctly, in due proportion; regulate, rule, govern, manage.* In these moments, I have lost my hold on that word. I have fucked all of the proportions right up.

Resolution: *the reduction or separation of an object or substance into constituent parts or elements.*

When I learned about the theory of humorism in some college class or other, I was hit with a wave of longing—if only it could really be that simple! A quick crash course: ancient Greek physicians held that people's temperaments were governed by the four bodily humors—blood, yellow bile, black bile, and phlegm. If the humors were in balance—if they were, in other words, *tempered*—then the person was healthy. But if one humor was more prominent than the others, that person's physical and/or emotional health suffered. Someone with an overabundance of yellow bile was *choleric*: hotheaded, quick to anger and to react. Too much black bile meant *melancholic*: moody, someone who broods and stews and frets. Yellow bile was understood to be produced by the gallbladder, black bile by the spleen. Someone rude and sharp-tongued has *got some gall*. Someone who lashes out is *venting her spleen*. The definitions and organ attributions blur and shift over the centuries. What stays consistent is the bile: necessary in proper moderation, but always acidic.

What a relief it would be, I thought, if someone could measure my humors, make the proper adjustments, temper me.

Even on tough days, we sort out our family squabbles—sometimes quickly, sometimes slowly, but always before sleep. If I've been snappish, if I've raised my voice, I say I'm sorry. I'm trying to teach my sons that people make mistakes, that moods are difficult, that apologies are important.

Still.

On nights when I've lost my temper, I've gone to bed feeling a little ill at how I've shifted the balance of my household, mired all of us temporarily in some queasy blend of anger and guilt and sulking. And on those nights, my comfort has been the likelihood of tomorrow. No tomorrow is guaranteed, of course, but most likely we'll all wake in the morning and I'll have another chance. On those nights, I resolve to temper myself. To work to be more *sanguine*—warm like the blood, ruled by the heart. Or, at the very least, more *phlegmatic*—calm, cool, governed by the brain. It feels good, making that resolution. It helps.

Resolution: *the alteration of a discord, or relatively dissonant harmony, so as to form a concord, or relatively more consonant harmony.*

When I was young, I contracted mononucleosis, which causes, among other ailments, a swollen spleen. I missed a full month of fourth grade and spent that time watching *Hogan's Heroes* and *I Dream of Jeannie* on the rust-colored velour couch. In 1 percent of mono cases, the spleen bursts. Mine did not, though for a month after I returned to school I was required to sit inside during recess to reduce the risk of splenic rupture.

The spleen is an important organ but not, it turns out, an essential one. Although its removal leaves patients at a higher risk of contracting infections, with care and luck one can live a long and happy spleenless life.

New Year's resolutions are notoriously difficult to keep: too big, too unwieldy, too much pressure. One year in my twenties, in an attempt to set an achievable resolution, I vowed to try an olive—something I'd managed my whole life to avoid—if I happened to be in a social setting where olives were available. I'm pretty sure it's the only New Year's resolution I've ever kept. At a party that February, I was sitting on a red loveseat when someone set a platter of cheese and olives right in front of me. I took a bite of a green olive. It was salty, and sharply pungent, and I didn't like it and discarded the rest of it uneaten on my plate, but I had kept my resolution. I felt unreasonably pleased with myself.

My kids like hearing that story—the year their mom made a funny resolution, one that holds none of the weight resolutions are supposed to hold. But I was able to keep that resolution, not because it was small or silly, though of course it was; I was able to keep it because all it required of me was trying.

Resolution: *dispersal or dissolution of humors or morbid material; softening of a hardened mass in the body; an instance of this. Obsolete.*

Outside our car that March evening, the sky was gray, heavy, sloping toward night; the road was congested with our small town's half-hearted 5 P.M. traffic. Outside our car, it was the opposite of celebration. But inside our car, from the back seat, my son said again, "Seriously, why can't we say 'Happy New Year' all the time?" Then, before I could answer, he shouted, "Happy New Year!" and his brother shouted, "Happy New Year!" in return. Warmth flooded my limbs against the late winter chill. An influx of sanguinity; my blood, for this moment, the predominating humor. My son was right, of course—this moment is a new year, and this moment, and this. So many chances to try. The steering wheel was cool under my hands, and I drove us slowly, carefully, home.

What We Found

6:00 P.M.

BY THE FIFTH HUNDRED-DEGREE DAY IN A ROW, I was desperate to get out to air and trees and cicadas. And so, when the sky clouded over after dinner, I told my youngest to put on his shoes—we were going for a walk. "Okay," he said, "but I want to go somewhere we've never been before." He was hoping, I think, for an actual New Place, somewhere exotic and beautiful, somewhere with mountains and temperatures in the mid-sixties and maybe Cheetos.

"Well," I said, "I guess we can turn right at the end of the street instead of left like we usually do." And being an unusually amenable five-year-old, my son agreed.

Outside, the air was still thick and heavy as a damp towel, but the clouds kept us covered and we began our explorations, my son picking up feathers and acorns and seedpods and cicada shells as we made our way to the New Street I'd promised. And as we turned onto it, I began to hear a buzzing sound. It paused for a moment, then started up again, faintly. Bees, I thought, and scanned the treetops for the swarming that would mean a nest. Other than a few cardinals, though, there was nothing.

We kept walking. The air was silent for a few more seconds, then broken again by the buzzing, closer now. A stop-and-start sound, and my brain landed on the next most reasonable explanation: someone was doing yard work on this street, using a Weedwacker, or maybe a chain saw.

Then the shrieking started. First the buzzing, louder now, then, immediately, a child's shriek. Then a pause. Then the buzzing, then the shrieking again. The ominous causality dawned on me slowly, like when you're watching what you think is a dark comedy and realize midway through that you're in for straight horror. What was happening here? Who was making this child scream? An angry parent threatening with a power tool? An older sibling, a babysitter, ready to teach a kid a lesson? What nightmare had my neighborhood morphed into?

But it made sense to me, too. It fit. Not given my neighborhood itself, which is generally quiet and friendly, full of waving neighbors and occasional rooster crowings. But given the world as we know it. Given the year, the year before that, the year before that, the shootings, the rage rallies, the day-to-day high alert, the half-mast flags, the minute-by-minute cruelties, the shocks that have ceased to be shocking, given this place and what it can hold—what else could it possibly be?

I scanned the street, the yards. Should I do something? Could I? What? My phone was in my hand, but what would I say? The buzzing got louder, got louder, the shrieking, too, and then I saw a child running around the side of a house and my heart revved.

Then I saw what he was running from. Another child walked into the side yard with a bright yellow toy trombone the color of a daffodil. As I watched, this child played a long, toneless *blat* at the first child, who shrieked again and ran. It was ridiculous. It was impossible. It was, in this moment, exactly what was happening. I remembered that children also shriek from delight. That sometimes things seem impossible because they are absurd and hilarious instead of unthinkably cruel.

I stared for a minute, reeling inside this reminder, until a neighbor recognized us and walked over to say hi, and she and I talked about the heat and humidity while my son found some tiny powder-blue berries, a metallic-green beetle. Behind us the kids yelled and blatted at each other.

After a while, my son and I walked home in the heat and I helped him carry what he'd found. Some of it was dead, and some of it might have been poisonous, but the berries were so blue, the feather so soft, the seedpods so mysteriously smooth. Somehow, though our hands were overflowing, we managed to hold all of it.

The Apologetic Body

7:00 P.M.

IN THE WEEKS IMMEDIATELY FOLLOWING MY FIRST son's birth, I experienced plenty of things I'd expected, at least in the abstract: a previously unmapped wilderness of love to navigate for this new human; exhaustion so disorienting my kitchen felt like the moon; the frightening weirdnesses of my healing and feeding and shrinking and expanding body.

One thing no book or blog had prepared me for, though, was the complete loss of any sense of embarrassment. As in, it entirely—*poof!*—disappeared.

It started, I suppose, with the pregnancy itself, all those months of offering up my body to hands and instruments, needles and monitors, in preparation for what would come next. And then, of course, there was the delivery, during which two nurses and a doctor coached me through pushing and reached into my body and helped usher out a yowling baby, all under glaring hospital lights. Though I cringed inwardly sometimes at all this unnatural intimacy, I rolled with it. My ability to manage those moments made sense to me. They, after all, were what came along with the version of pregnancy and birth I'd decided I wanted.

What I didn't expect was what happened a few hours after my son was born. By seven in the evening, those blurred first hours and their requirements over, the three of us—the three of us!—were in our hospital room, stunned and blissed out. My husband and I played music softly on the phone while our baby got used to nursing. I had my hospital gown down around my waist so our son could latch on while resting warm against my skin. The door opened, and in came my mother and stepfather, just arrived after their through-the-night drive from Delaware to Mississippi.

"Oh!" cried my mother, seeing her grandson for the first time. Then—"Oh!" as she realized I was pretty much naked and would surely be embarrassed with all this sudden company. My stepfather immediately averted his eyes as he tried simultaneously to convey his congratulatory happiness.

"It's fine," I said, "I'm just feeding the baby," and made no effort to cover any part of myself, because why in the world would I? I felt no embarrassment, no awkwardness. Nor did I feel indignation. I felt the facts: I had just given birth. I was a mother now. I was feeding my boy from my own body. Could I be as naked as I pleased? Damn right. And because I was so secure in my awareness of these miracles, I carried on a lovely and completely gone-from-memory conversation with my mother and stepfather and husband for, apparently, quite some time while I sat there in the almost altogether, and because I was so completely okay with it, everyone else had to pretend to be too.

What a relief it was, not to care! What a relief to do exactly what needed to be done, to do what I *knew* needed to be done, to know that I could make that decision and everyone around me would accept it—because what choice did they have?

Two nights later, we were home, trying to figure out how we were supposed to take care of this surprisingly complicated small person. He woke almost constantly. He ate almost constantly. He required diaper changes almost constantly. At midnight, my husband and I were both up, trying to solve the logistics of the pajamas, the onesie snaps, the diaper, the wipes. We hadn't yet learned the crucial trick of always having a spare washcloth handy as a shield when changing a baby boy, and as we were fumbling around, slow in our sleep-deprived addledness, our son peed an impressive arc up over his own head and onto the wall behind him. My husband and I stared in amazement. And then we started laughing. And I kept laughing. It was the kind of laughing that opens and opens and opens. It was the kind of laughing that says *I've been through something and now I'm here and I'm so glad*. I laughed and laughed, and then, because two days earlier I'd pushed a baby out of my body using muscles I hadn't known I had, I peed right down my legs. I couldn't help it. It wasn't a lot, but it was enough, and as I said to my husband, "Oh, shit, I just peed myself!" I started laughing harder. I couldn't stop laughing. It is one of my favorite memories from those early days.

During my pregnancy, I had researched all of the many ways that childbirth can wreak havoc on a mother's body. Abdominal separation, uterine prolapse, hair loss, hemorrhoids, night sweats, blood clots, chronic pain—the list is endless and overwhelming. Incontinence—temporary or permanent—is one of the more common postbirth side effects, and it was one of the many things I'd fretted about. What if that happened to me? How terrible not to be in control of my own body; how mortifying. But when it happened, that first night home from the hospital, it was like my fears had existed in a different story, a parallel world. It didn't matter now. Probably this wasn't permanent (it wasn't), and I had a thousand more crucial things to focus on, and the laughter was such a relief after all the months of worry and waiting. I didn't even consider trying to hide what had happened from my husband. I wasn't embarrassed because I had no room for embarrassment. Various states had jockeyed for a place in my brain, and the strongest few had won out: Vast Love, Exhaustion, Worry, and Getting Shit Done. Embarrassment, that little simperer, had been kicked to the curb. It wasn't even difficult, I realized. Embarrassment had always been delicate.

I existed in this blissful state for another week or so. I talked candidly with everyone about my difficulties breastfeeding and the surprising goriness of my body's healing. I walked around half clothed, joked about perching on the edges of chairs because I couldn't yet sit. It was a kind of high, this unanticipated and absolute release from inhibition.

I'd never considered how exhausting it is to have a body and pretend it requires nothing. I'd never thought about the day-to-day work it takes to consistently execute the impossible restraint our culture dictates as the norm—to stop crying when someone approaches, to think about our fears and impolite hilarities but not discuss them, to care for our hurting or healing or wounded bodies secretly so no one is bothered. And I'd never considered, not really, the tremendous amount of embarrassment—and, with it, guilt—that many of us carry around daily because of our bodies and their needs. If we have to cancel plans due to illness or exhaustion or a flare-up of pain, we apologize. If our brains need medicine to achieve a better balance, we might keep it quiet. If we need someone to accompany us to a doctor's appointment—to drive, or maybe just because we're anxious and would like company—we feel bad for inconveniencing. If menstrual blood stains the sheets, we're abashed. If our bodies don't present as somehow Correct, the narrative tells us we must be doing something wrong. We're sorry we're too fatigued to bring cupcakes. We're sorry our body did that thing, sorry it looks this way, sorry we made your child ask an awkward question. We're sorry we're ill. We're sorry we're injured. We're sorry that someday we'll die and leave more people inconvenienced. We're sorry, we're sorry, we're sorry. It's a wonder we don't all spontaneously combust.

I say this, too, as someone speaking from a position of serious body privilege: I'm a woman, which is a strike against me, and I'm over forty, which is another, but otherwise, as a white, thin, cisgender person without visible disabilities and with access to and means for health care, I check most of the boxes for moving as smoothly as possible through this world. Even with this privilege, that handful of days when I didn't feel like I had to reconcile my body's needs with the world's comfort was a massive, massive relief.

I'm sure it was at least partly the oxytocin—the so-called love hormone released during and after childbirth—that spurred me into this particular state of utter freedom, and maybe also just the epiphanic reseeing that can happen after a life's sea change. Whatever the cause, during those blurred days, that relief was the opposite of blurring. It was a snapping-into-focus. An instant prioritizing. A clarifying, precise and crystalline. If I was up with the baby at 3 A.M. and wanted leftover quiche from the fridge, I ate the quiche. When my bra made my breasts ache, I didn't wear a bra. I couldn't eat at the table because sitting was too painful, so I ate lying on the couch. I was thirsty in the middle of nursing, so I asked for water and someone brought it to me. My fluctuating hormones made me want to cry all the time, so I cried all the time—into my cereal, into my baby's hair—and didn't apologize for it. What my body needed, I gave it. This, too, was possible because of privilege: my husband, a professor like me, was able to be home during those early days, which happened to coincide with our winter break. My mother and stepfather both managed to take time off work to come help. And I had three weeks before I needed to be out in the world again in any way. So when I needed to cry, I was in my home and not my office. It took weeks for me to sit comfortably, but someone else could drive to the grocery store, to CVS, so I could avoid the pain of climbing into the car, navigating the gas pedal and brake. When I needed something to drink, all I had to do was ask. I had every single blessing a person could hope to have.

Even still—even with all of this—it was almost impossible.

Imagine if everyone who had given birth could take paid parental leave. Imagine if partners could do the same to support their healing loved ones. Now keep going. Imagine affordable, unstigmatized treatment for everything from postpartum depression to nursing woes to pelvic-floor prolapse. Imagine if every person who needed care could feel safe in seeking it. Imagine if every person who needed to stay home and recover—from childbirth or COVID or surgery or a mental-health crisis or a chronic illness flare or a run-of-the-mill virus contagious to everyone in the workspace—could do so without fear of losing their livelihood. Imagine how much healthier we'd all be. How much better all of our bodies would feel.

The elation of jettisoning all embarrassment didn't last, of course. By the end of the month, the new chemicals racing around my system had leveled out, and I was back to a more standard sense of reserve and decorum—wearing clothes when I was expected to, avoiding talk about bodily viscera in polite company. It was natural, this shift back into the social world, but it was also a loss. That utter freedom had been a kind of magic. A lifting. A lofting. Its vanishing was a quiet, if necessary, sadness.

But it didn't vanish altogether. Just as pregnant mothers permanently take on some of their babies' fetal cells, I'm still carrying some measure of what I honed postpartum. After decades of mistaking my own shame for politeness, I've started asking for what I need when I need it: help with carrying the car seat when I'm wrangling two kids solo onto a plane. An afternoon nap when I can feel tiredness becoming exhaustion. More fiber. More cherries. Zoloft.

Or, say I decided to write about embarrassment. Long ago, I would have said, *What are you doing, mentioning the nakedness, the incontinence, the Zoloft? Your body is all over this page!* Now I'd answer, Damn right.

The Idea of It: Three Countries

8:00 P.M.

1. Italy

When I set out for Florence, the contents of my backpack were ridiculous: three E. M. Forster novels (two about Tuscany), brand-new green Converse, clothes appropriate to the soft and golden clime I imagined I'd find in Italy during March. I hadn't researched the weather. I didn't pack a water bottle. I didn't pack an umbrella. I didn't pack nearly enough socks for the three weeks I'd be traveling around the country.

I wasn't worried. I was twenty. I had *Roman Holiday* memorized. I'd seen *The English Patient* three times in the theater. I knew what to expect: fountains and motorbikes and a charming man broodily buying me grappa. Earlier that year, while still at my small Pennsylvania college, I'd spent entire class periods staring blankly at chalkboards while my brain zoomed around villas.

The trip, of course, went exactly the way you'd expect it to go for someone who'd expected foolishly. How I came down with a wicked fever on the overnight train my friend Sarah and I took from Paris to Florence. How it drizzled for the first nine days we were there. How one morning I gorged myself on fresh-baked bread, thinking I'd gain strength, like Heidi in the Alps, and ended up so nauseous that for a week I had to cross streets to avoid bakery aromas. How my new sneakers blistered my heels. How I stumbled over the words I hadn't bothered to learn before arriving. How our one potential romantic rendezvous ended abruptly when the guys, two Pennsylvanians we'd met promisingly (Grand Canal, rainstorm), started making gay jokes and we caught the next water taxi back to the hostel.

There were, of course, villas and fountains. There were motorbikes and tubs of gelato and absurdly beautiful stone towers, and as the days went on there was increasing sun and warmth, and we found an alley in Verona where tiny white lights draped over our heads like an awning. Everything looked like the movies, even in the rain. The trouble was the script. I'd imagined Italy as a backdrop to my unfolding cinematic narrative. I hadn't considered that I was an extra in a film already long in progress.

2. Road Trip USA

The summer after we both turned twenty-three, my oldest friend Emily and I embarked on a cross-country road trip. We'd both grown up in the suburbs of Wilmington, Delaware, thirty minutes from Philadelphia, smack in the middle of bustling and generic East Coast strip mall land. We were ready for mountains. We were ready for diners. We were ready for Americana.

In Oklahoma, we found ourselves tooling slowly down the main street of a small town, with the sort of old storefronts and marquees that hinted at a decades-past heyday. Now, twenty years later, I know many of these towns; I live near several of them, bought my dining room light fixture in the one down the road. At the time, though, this was brand new to both of us, wild and quaint, like a ghost town where people still lived. It felt like stepping into the past, and we were all about time travel.

As we drove, we kept our eyes out for a café or coffee shop, somewhere to grab a bite to tide us over until dinner a few hundred miles later. Then we saw the sign for the drive-in restaurant. We couldn't believe it—a real 1950s-style drive-in, with milkshakes and burgers and fountain Cokes. It hadn't even been listed in the *Let's Go* travel guide we'd been using. We'd discovered a secret.

"Where *are* we?" I whispered, awestruck, by which I meant, *When* are we?

"Right?" replied Emily, wide eyed.

We couldn't get over our luck, the wonder of our find. We ordered through the speaker, and when our milkshakes and fries were delivered, we snapped pictures of each other so that we could show our friends what we'd found, out there in the forgotten stretches of the country.

An hour later, back on the highway, sated and delighted, we passed a highway exit sign listing food and lodging options. Days Inn, Ramada. McDonald's, Wendy's, Subway, Sonic.

We both saw it. "Wait," Emily said, at the same time I said, "Wait," and then we both said, "Oh my god" and "Oh my god we took pictures" and "Oh my god we're such idiots" and "Oh my god" and "Oh my god" and "Oh my god."

It was true that Sonic hadn't yet come to New York, where Emily lived, or to Columbus, Ohio, where I'd been living. We hadn't heard of it, had no idea drive-in restaurants were still—or newly—operating. On the other hand, it sure had looked exactly like a fast-food chain, down to its font and branded cups and prices. We realized all of this in the moment we passed the green exit sign. But until then, we'd discovered something. Until then, we were in a different story.

3. Motherhood

One night when our son was about a week old, my husband and I decided to read him his first bedtime story. Thanks to exhaustion, the hours of the day had become strange and unreal, and it seemed like a good idea to begin implementing a solid eight o'clock bedtime routine. More than that, though: after a week of constant small failures—I could not master the breastfeeding "football hold," I was clumsy at giving him his baths, my body wasn't healing as quickly as I thought it should—I was desperate to do the one thing I had absolute confidence I could do. Here was a moment I'd thought about for decades. When I pictured "parenting," I pictured reading to my child. I knew I'd do it well. I knew I'd do it right.

I plucked *The Tale of Squirrel Nutkin,* one of several lovely hardbound Beatrix Potter books a friend had given us, off the neatly arranged shelf in the nursery. My husband and I nestled our son between us in bed and I started reading.

Realizations I came to quickly:

The Tale of Squirrel Nutkin is very long.

The Tale of Squirrel Nutkin is kind of terrifying.

Perhaps most obvious of all to anyone who has ever been around a baby: one-week-olds are not good story listeners.

But my husband and I would have this moment, damn it, our son sweetly cradled between us as we read to him. I'd planned this memory. We'd look back on this misty-eyed, remembering the two of us exhausted but glad, our infant in his dark blue onesie with peace signs all over it, this first story, this foray into the wide and wild world of reading we'd impart to him.

Our son squawked. He arched his back.

"But Nutkin was excessively impertinent in his manners," I read, a bit louder. "He bobbed up and down like a little red cherry, singing—"

Our son began to fuss, rooting his small face toward me, hungry again.

"*Riddle me, riddle me, rot-tot-tote!*" I read. "*A little wee man, in a red red coat! A staff in his hand, and a stone in his throat; If you'll tell me this riddle, I'll give you a groat.*"

"What's a groat?" my husband asked.

"I don't know," I said, at which point our son began a full-throated cry. I gave up, propping myself on pillows to nurse again, laying the book face down and open to the page where we'd left off, though my husband and I both knew we'd never return to it. I was embarrassed. I'd failed in this most classic of parental moments. And I was unmoored, suddenly deeply, unreservedly sad. If I couldn't succeed at reading a story to my child—the one thing I felt completely qualified to do, the one thing I really *knew*—how in the world could I expect to do anything else correctly?

4. Italy

Verona was the second-to-last stop on our trip. By then Sarah and I were weary of our travel book and its exhortations. We'd seen the Uffizi, we'd toured the Sistine Chapel, we'd climbed Siena's tower. On our first night in Verona, we walked around aimlessly until we came to a luxe bakery. We went in, bought a fancy chocolate ganache cake in lieu of dinner, and then sat by a fountain and ate the whole thing with our hands.

The next day, we happened upon Giardino Giusti, a large, beautiful garden near the center of the city. We hadn't read about it; we hadn't been looking for it. But there it was, its sculptured topiaries spiking into the sky, its lawns lush and green. At a nearby grocery store we bought crackers and a big bottle of what we called rosé but which was, we later realized, a jug of cooking wine, which explained the gentle laughter from the old lady waiting in line behind us, who surely understood the whole scene. We snuck all of it into the garden and spent the day snacking, writing poems, sharing headphones to listen to Bob Dylan, drinking from our jug. We got a little drunk, or we thought we did. When we had to pee, one of us stood guard while the other disappeared behind a shrub. We wrote letters to people we loved and either sent them or lost our nerve; I forget now. It was the writing that was important. We talked and talked about graduation, about what would be next, where we'd live, with whom. We talked about if we'd ever make it back to Italy. I didn't know someday I'd live in Mississippi. I didn't know I'd marry someone I hadn't yet met, a fiction writer I'd think about a few years later while on a cross-country road trip with Emily. I didn't know I'd have two sons who'd grow to love stories, who'd curl against me each night to read about dragons and pigs and dog rescues in the Alps. In that Veronese garden, maybe half drunk on cooking wine, I didn't know what to expect. Everything was possible, and then some of it happened.

Company

9:00 P.M.

I TOOK A BREATH AND TRIED TO GAUGE IF THE very top of my right lung ached more or less than it had the day before. Maybe less this time? I took another breath, a deep one, and grimaced. Not less. Or maybe? It didn't hurt a lot—hardly at all—but I shouldn't be aware of what it felt like to breathe, right? And the kids—what had they eaten for breakfast? How had they slept? What were they wearing today? Also I had been coughing a lot in the mornings, and I always coughed a lot in the mornings, but was this *more* coughing? Different coughing? *Was* I feeling something in my lung, or was this my mind going rogue again? I didn't know, I didn't know. I was adrift in all my not-knowing.

Outside my studio window, a groundhog trundled cheerfully across the grass. The midmorning September sun sang gold over the wild meadows beyond. Nothing was required of me here. The whole day—the whole night, if I wanted—was mine for writing and reading. An impossible gift in an impossibly beautiful place.

On my desk, the stack of poetry books I'd brought with me, still unread. My laptop, open not to a draft but to tabs from the Mayo Clinic on lung cancer symptoms, the American Cancer Society on cancer rates by type, and the Cleveland Clinic on pulmonary embolism diagnosis, plus an Excel spreadsheet where I'd tried to math myself into reassurance by calculating likelihoods based on age and risk factors. I thought of the kids at school, seven hundred miles away, back home in Mississippi—did they have their water bottles? Hoodies? I took another breath. It hurt a little, just enough that I knew I would inhale deeply one more time to see how that one felt. Then one more time. The groundhog ambled back the other way, unconcerned. Fucking groundhog.

In retrospect, I should have known better. I talk a lot in my classes about the individuality of the creative process, how writing isn't a one-size-fits-all pursuit. I talk about the bullshit notion that you're only a writer if you write every day, and how that belief is deeply steeped in a history of privilege. I tell my students about how my own writing practice has shifted and evolved as my life has shifted and evolved. I emphasize how important it is to be patient with yourself, to stay attuned to your own needs as a writer and human and do what you can to advocate for those needs.

And I *know* my own needs as a writer and human. I've always felt healthiest and most creative when I'm required to be a person in the world. Before I had kids I used to teach every summer in addition to all school year long—to make extra money, sure, but also because I knew my brain needed that daily structure. I was afraid to leave it unchaperoned all through those hot summer months. I thrive on connection. I thrive, as much as I sometimes wish it weren't the case, on responsibility, tasks, daily life.

I know all of this. And yet, when my kids were five and eight and I had finally emerged from the chaos of the baby days, and most things were humming along at a steady if sometimes frantic pace—I decided it was time to try a writing residency. I'd never done one. Before kids I hadn't felt the need, and after kids I hadn't felt I could or should. But now the time seemed right. I wanted, after years of often putting my work as a writer behind my work as a mother or teacher or errand-running member of a household unit, to see what I could do if I became, even for just a little while, the kind of writer who was *all in*, who prioritized brainspace and time and gave herself completely over to craft.

So I applied for a residency, and was thrilled when I received the email inviting me to spend a week. I'd heard from other writer friends about the magical productivity they'd been able to access in this particular place—in private studios surrounded by rolling green mountains, boxwoods, and fields—and couldn't wait to give myself permission, for seven whole days, to be only and entirely a writer.

When I arrived, the natural beauty lived up to my expectations. There were small white butterflies everywhere, and wild gardens full of willows and sculptures and bottlebrush buckeye.

At night the stars spilled out over the vast, dark sky. The quiet was staggering. The circumstances were primed for Maximum Creativity.

More specifically, the circumstances were primed for somebody else's Maximum Creativity. Soon after arrival, it became clear that I wasn't going to be able to access the verdant mental space I'd imagined slipping into. As I'd known but tried to forget, extended time with only my own thoughts for company has never gone well for me, and this week was no exception. I tried to write, managed to get down a few rough beginnings, but my mind wanted to focus not on language and line breaks but on the fallibility of my body. After a bout with pneumonia some months back, my obsessive worry had found a new locus in my lungs, and all that time alone meant plenty of hours to listen to my own breathing in my studio's silence. My brain felt jittery, a nervous colt bucking at concentration's halter.

Compounding everything was my awareness that this wasn't likely to be an opportunity I'd have again. We'd budgeted for this week, worked out childcare and kids' schedules, and generally moved some heavy pieces to make this possible, and guilt clanked around in my mind each time I stared blankly at my laptop screen, typing and then deleting words. I had this one incredible opportunity—and I was blowing it.

Most powerfully of all, though: I missed my family, my husband and our sons, with an acuteness that startled me. I'd traveled solo before, of course, and I'd missed them on those occasions and had anticipated missing them now, but here, alone in my studio, alone in my bedroom, alone walking down the gravel path at twilight, I missed them fervently. This was the longest I'd ever been away from the boys. All I wanted was to hear their voices. All I wanted was to sit on their floor as they fell asleep.

One evening around nine, midway through the week, another writer and I were picking our way through the dark from our private studios to our private sleeping quarters when she told me that the cottage she'd been assigned felt spooky at night.

"Maybe it's haunted," I said, joking.

But as the words left my mouth, a wave of jealousy sloshed over me. In my own quiet room there was no one and nothing but me. I wanted companionship, interruptions, noise. I wanted to be woken in the night, wanted to be jostled and nudged, wanted dropped dishes, mysterious spills. I wanted someone to need me, to not leave me alone. I missed my sons, their endless energy, their questions, the urgency of their ping-ponging moods. I missed my husband. I missed *my* people, the ones who knew me better than anyone, the ones around whom I never felt awkward. And I missed, I realized, knowing that no matter how deep I dove into my thoughts, at 2:30 P.M. I'd need to swim back up to the sunlight and get in the carpool lane. That quick burst back to the surface hurt sometimes—the psychological bends—but it also helped me be a person. Here, right now, in this lovely, peaceful place, I didn't feel like much of a person, and certainly not like much of a writer. I did need time, and quiet, and brainspace, I absolutely did, often more than I got at home. But I needed it all in balance with everything else. And since balance was—is—impossible, I realized that what I needed was all of it—time and quiet and brainspace and soccer practice and shoe meltdowns and bedtime stories and stacks of student papers and department meetings and blueberries and old-fashioneds and late nights and early mornings and exhaustion and complaining about exhaustion and birthday parties and books of poems and books of dinosaurs and books of Russian aristocracy and books of cartoon dogs fighting robot villains and books upon books upon books I'd lament never having time to read, and haircuts and full moons and popcorn on the green couch—in whatever messy, maddening configuration I could swing.

As I crunched along the gravel path with the writer who had a probable ghost waiting to greet her, my jealousy startled me, showing up like it did out of nowhere, slipping through the walls of my consciousness. I could feel it just over my shoulder. No one else could see it, but I knew it was there, reminding me of who I was and what I needed. *You're not an all-in writer,* it murmured in its soft spectral voice, polite but direct. *Admit it. Go ahead and miss everyone.* My own ghost stayed with me the rest of the week, hovering close as I ate and wrote and hiked and slept. Eventually I became comfortable with it, this little specter of longing. It stayed beside me until I went home, and I was grateful for its company.

Foxes

10:00 P.M.

WHEN THE LITTLE ONE WAS VERY LITTLE, HE didn't like to fall asleep by himself. He liked to chat and ask for water and kick his blanket off and request that it be pulled back up. He liked company as he talked with his animals or recited books or sang Heart's "Barracuda." And his two-hour preschool naps meant he stayed up late. Most nights it was nine thirty or ten before he was out, and then I was emerging blinking and mole-eyed into the kitchen, already half in dreams, no longer at all equipped to grade papers or answer emails or curl on the couch with my husband and a beer. So it was understandable, I think, that I got a little impatient sometimes, sitting in the rocking chair in the dark, night-lighted room, waiting for him to give in to sleep.

When he was very little, he slept with two cats, three dogs, a possum, two bears, and two foxes. The stuffed cats slept snuggled with him, and the other animals usually got relegated to the foot of the bed. But one night, as I sat in his chair, he reached down and brought both foxes up to the place of honor.

He talked to them for a bit, and I zoned out, as I often do, thinking about grading or rising sea levels or how I might need jaw surgery, and then after a while he got quiet, and I waited for his breathing to shift into the steady heaviness that means sleep. It felt like we'd been silent for a long time, and then he said, "Mommy?"

Oh no, I thought. *We were almost there.* "Yeah, honey?" I said. I braced myself for a water request. A snack lamentation. A sock situation. Anything that would start the whole cycle over again.

"I wish there could be plenty of foxes for everybody," he said. And what else is there to say about that, other than that the world stopped for a split second and flipped the other way on its axis and gravity disappeared and everything filled with stars, and then we were back in the quiet bedroom, and I said, "Me too," and after a while his breathing slowed and deepened into sleep.

Accomplishment

11:00 P.M.

THE AMOUNT OF JOY I GOT FROM THE THOUSAND-piece puzzle, a Christmas gift from my father, was unfathomable. I still can't pinpoint the exact provenance of my gladness. Certainly it had to do with color: hundreds of animal species rendered in vivid shade and detail, starting with the humpback red snapper in the top left corner and arcing through the rainbow palette until reaching the forest mother-of-pearl butterfly, elegant in its shimmering violet, in the lower right. It had to do with the quality of the puzzle, its subtle gloss, the heft of the pieces in my fingers. It had to do with the animals themselves, so many whose names I'd never heard (golden mantella, hieroglyphic moth, Siamese fireback). But mainly, I think, it had to do with Accomplishing Something.

When I opened the puzzle, it had been nine months since I'd last taught a class in person. Nine months since my kids had gone to school anywhere other than at the kitchen table or their bedroom desk. Nine months of vigilance and a queasy miasma of sadness and anger and disbelief and worry humming constantly in my head. Nine months since I'd had the kind of day I used to have often—a day when I'd get up, shower, take the kids to school, walk two miles around the campus lake, buy coffee, and be seated at my desk in my office by 8:30 A.M. I'd fill those days with a thousand Things. I'd answer emails. I'd prep for classes. I'd walk across campus, teach, walk back, eat lunch. I'd revise a poem I'd started the week before. I'd begin drafting a new poem. I'd teach another class. Answer some more emails. Then lock my office door and drive to my kids' after-school program, where I'd pick them up and hear all about their days and try to put my attention fully on them despite not having gotten enough done.

What in the world was I trying to accomplish in those days? How were those eight hours not enough? Eight hours of time, of quiet, of checking off. By the late December afternoon when I began working on the puzzle, I was lucky to take a shower most days of the week. I, like everyone I knew, was drowning in emails. I was behind on all but the most essential aspects of my job. I had written a few new poems since everything had shut down in March, but hadn't sent them out. My kids spent too much time on screens. I was with them all the time, and not with them enough. I was doing everything—parenting, teaching, writing, being a wife and friend and daughter—just passably, and doing nothing well.

But the puzzle. The gorgeous puzzle with its colors and creatures and perfect-fit pieces. With its blue morpho, green peafowl, red panda. Every night I could sit at my kitchen table after the kids went to sleep and snap more and more of it into place. And every time I found the right piece—every time—I accomplished something.

It became addictive. I worked on the puzzle while my kids were playing video games. I worked on the puzzle long after my husband had gone to bed, telling him I'd be back in a few minutes but unwilling to climb down from the high I felt with every completed blue tail feather, every green claw. As I neared the end of the puzzle, I became territorial, like the fennec fox in the upper right quadrant. I stopped working on it when the kids were awake. I told my husband I wanted to do it myself (I get it, said my husband, and I believe he actually did, which is one of the many reasons I'm lucky).

And then, one night—everyone else in bed and long asleep, even the dog—I finished the puzzle. It was beautiful, and bright, and complete. In the silent house I ran my hands over the puzzle's smoothness. After eight days of work, I had done it. I had started something, and then I had finished it.

I took a deep breath and let it out. The year. The franticness. The constant worry. The interruptions and interruptions and interruptions of everything. The green of the tiger beetle. The gold of the kinkajou. My children were in bed, safe, and I had made something. I touched the puzzle again. Then I broke it apart—carefully, tenderly—and boxed it up, piece by gleaming piece.

Animals

12:00 A.M.

I'M AWAKE IN BED, WITH MY HUSBAND ASLEEP next to me and the dog even more deeply asleep next to me, listening to mysterious animal sounds in the woods behind our backyard when it strikes me: this is the house my kids are growing up in. I know this sounds like a nonrealization—like, of course it is, yes, and also they like to eat pancakes for breakfast, and also the grass is green. But it hits me hard and fast, this realization which is not a non-realization at all. This is the house my kids are growing up in. This is it, it's happening, right now. It's not something that's someday *going* to happen. It's happening. It started happening without ceremony, without signal. I hadn't thought about it until this moment, lying awake, gazing without my glasses at the blurred rectangle of light that I know is the window glowing from our cul-de-sac's streetlamp. This is the house they'll remember, just like I remember my own house, the townhouse on Opal Court, the blurred rectangle of light in my own bedroom at night, the rust-colored living room couch, the TV on the white-painted bookcase that wasn't intended as a

TV stand and always teetered just enough to be nerve-wracking, just like I remember the corner where the Christmas tree stood and the month I had mono and watched reruns of *Hogan's Heroes* and *I Dream of Jeannie* on the rust-colored couch and the ripple of thrill and shame I felt when a boy came over to give me earrings and they were nice earrings but the boy was the wrong boy, just like I remember the lemonade stand on our patio, how my mother froze cherries into ice cubes to make it fancy, and how my father and I used to play Contra on the Nintendo after my homework was done, and the tadpole named Brett who lived in a murky tank on my dresser until he died when we were away for a weekend and the neighbor brought him to me in a Ziploc bag and how even though I hadn't really loved Brett I wept and wept because I knew what grief was supposed to look like, and how one night, nauseous with the anxiety I hadn't yet learned to name or quell, I puked into my hands and all over the newly painted yellow walls of my room, just like I remember sneaking my mother's Jackie Collins books from under her bed, just like I remember the cockapoo Wally who lived across the yard and liked to drink beer out of an ashtray, just like I remember nights reading *The Far Side* in bed and watching *The Jeffersons* in bed and thinking in bed about M, and M, and R, and N, and A, and every other boy I imagined kissing me or rescuing me from drowning or joining me in an impromptu musical performance of "Happy Together" as we sold pencils side by side at the school store, just like I remember, even still, my knifelike longing for the future, for a time when someone would kiss me, a time when my desires would make sense, a time when I would understand the jokes I heard on the bus and the sly asides in movies, a time when my hair wouldn't embarrass me, when my nose wouldn't embarrass me, when my voice wouldn't embarrass me—just like I remember all of that, all of it, just like all of that happened, now my kids' childhoods are happening, right now, in this place. My parents wanted to keep me safe and they did keep me safe, but they couldn't alter the way my brain churned, didn't know what I thought about in bed or in the back seat or on the bus, couldn't see or hear or understand everything, and I know now how that must have gnawed at them—*What don't we know?* they must have wondered, *How is this human we made so separate from us?* In eighth grade I was the first one home every day and would go into the basement and scream—a release for whatever had been pent up inside me throughout the middle school day, a moment of permission to the animal self I hid for every other hour. I remember that, too, just like I remember all the other secrets I kept, all the fears I never voiced, all the new and frightening and delightful thrills, all the questions upon questions that kept me up.

Now I am awake in the middle of the night on the first night of a new year, and in the woods behind the house animals are making sounds, and I don't know what the animals are. Later I'll Google it—*what animals make high-pitched sounds in the woods at night?*—but right now I am too distracted, too startled by this realization, this idea that my kids are in the middle of their own childhoods, vivid and confusing and everything-brand-new piquant like mine was, like childhoods are. It is jarring. It is both a terror and a relief—these lives, these lives that I can't fully know, these lives I want to keep safe, make easy, these lives that I can only guide so much. I am lying in bed thinking about all of this, and my eyes are open, wide open as next to me my husband and my dog breathe dreamingly. All I can see is the room's darkness, and then the rectangle of light. I listen to the animals in the woods, the animals I can't identify, their calls that aren't for me. I don't know what they're saying, but they are absorbed in their conversation. They are saying something urgent. They don't sound afraid.

Acknowledgments

THANK YOU TO THE EDITORS OF THE FOLLOWING publications where these essays first appeared, sometimes in different form.

Cincinnati Review, "What It Sounds Like"
Ecotone, "The Apologetic Body"
The New York Times, "Winter Work" (as "I Dreaded Winter Until My Newborn Taught Me to Embrace It")
River Teeth, "A Total Solar Eclipse Is Visible from Any Given Point on Earth Once Every 375 Years, on Average"
Tupelo Quarterly, "Perfect Sentence"
Waxwing, "What We Found"

The poem "Cardinal Virtue," quoted in "An Incomplete Catalog of My Vigilance," is from Nicky Beer's book *The Diminishing House.*

This book would never have made its way out into the world without the support, brilliance, and friendship of many, many people. My deepest gratitude:

To Nicky Beer & Brian Barker & Amy Wilkinson & Nathan Oates, for decades (!) of conversation, shenanigans, writerly advice, and cocktails, and in particular to Nicky and Amy for their sage feedback on these essays and deeply appreciated encouragement (also shenanigans).

To Emily Spivack and Ian Chillag, for conversation about art, essays, and parenting, and for always being up for Skee-Ball. Emily, there's no one with whom I'd rather have an embarrassing experience involving a Sonic—so grateful for the past thirty-five years (and counting) of our friendship.

To Maggie Smith, Aimee Nezhukumatathil, and Kathryn Nuernberger for their generosity and for the gift of their own essays and poems.

Thank you to my colleagues and students at Mississippi State University.

My family is the best family, and anything I've been able to accomplish is thanks to their love, guidance, and general coolness. Thank you to my mom, Debbie Albence, and my stepdad, Ron Albence, for driving through the night from Delaware to Mississippi *multiple times* to meet / care for / help with / hang out with our children, for making date nights possible, and for their love and encouragement, always. Mom, thank you for having my books on your bookshelf. Your support has given me the foundation for doing these things I love, and means the whole world to me. It always has.

Thank you to my dad, Carl Pierce, for always cheering me on, for letting my entire family—including the dog—crash at his house for months on end, and for his lifelong encouragement. Thank you, Dad, for teaching me, and then my kids, all of the important lessons and also some inappropriate words, and thank you for loving all of us so well.

Thank you to my sister, Sarah Reeder, for being sounding board and supporter, role model and friend, and thank you to Trevor, O, and E for making me laugh almost as hard as Sarah does.

Thank you to my entire family for a childhood filled with books and love, for encouraging me to write, always, and, when I told them I was going to be a creative writing major and a theater minor in college, for never, not even once, saying *But how will you make money?*

Thank you to Julie Kardos and the whole Kardos side of the family—I'm so lucky to have landed with you.

Thank you to agent extraordinaire Allison Malecha, for her brilliant insights into this book and how to make it better, and for being the greatest literary champion I could imagine. Thank you to Marisa Siegel for her belief in this book and for helping it to be the best possible version of itself. Thank you to the entire team at Northwestern University Press, including Madeline Schultz, Anne Gendler, and Megan Stielstra, for their skill, care, and kindness.

Thank you to Michael Kardos, who said *Keep going with these essays,* who said *So are you working toward a collection?,* who said *Go, work, get it done, I'll hold down the fort,* who believed in this book well before it was a book, who has believed in me ever since we were in grad school printing out submissions and sending them off with SASEs and then heading to Larry's for cheap beer and Cajun peanuts. Mike, this book wouldn't exist without you. Thank you for our life. Thank you for everything.

And to S and W—heart of this book, heart of my heart. Thank you for being your hilarious, thoughtful, questioning, adventurous, and utterly yourselves selves. I love you both immeasurably.